CAMPAIGN 293

DOWNFALL 1945

The Fall of Hitler's Third Reich

STEVEN J ZALOGA

ILLUSTRATED BY STEVE NOON
Series editor Marcus Cowper

First published in Great Britain in 2016 by Osprey Publishing,
PO Box 883, Oxford, OX1 9PL, UK
1385 Broadway, 5th Floor, New York, NY 10018, USA
E-mail: info@ospreypublishing.com

ISBN: 978 1 4728 1143 1
PDF e-book ISBN: 978 1 4728 1144 8
e-Pub ISBN: 978 1 4728 1145 5

Editorial by Ilios Publishing Ltd, Oxford, UK (www.iliospublishing.com)
Index by Fionbar Lyons
Typeset in Myriad Pro and Sabon
Maps by Bounford.com
3D bird's-eye views by The Black Spot
Battlescene illustrations by Steve Noon
Originated by PDQ Media, Bungay, UK
Printed in China through Worldprint Ltd.

16 17 18 19 20   10 9 8 7 6 5 4 3 2 1

ARTIST'S NOTE

Readers may care to note that the original paintings from which the color plates in this book were prepared are available for private sale. The Publishers retain all reproduction copyright whatsoever. All enquiries should be addressed to:

www.steve-noon.co.uk

The Publishers regret that they can enter into no correspondence upon this matter.

THE WOODLAND TRUST

Osprey Publishing are supporting the Woodland Trust, the UK's leading woodland conservation charity, by funding the dedication of trees.

AUTHOR'S NOTES

For brevity, the traditional conventions have been used when designating units. The US Army used Arabic numerals for divisions and smaller independent formations (9th Division, 756th Tank Battalion); Roman numerals for corps (VII Corps), spelled numbers for field armies (First US Army) and Arabic numerals for army groups (12th Army Group). British/Canadian practice was somewhat more flexible and the period practice was to use Arabic numerals for divisions and corps, and spelled numerals for armies. Soviet designations are all rendered in English since the Russian language is less familiar to most readers, so 5th Shock Army instead of "5-aya udarnaya armiya." The Red Army only used Arabic numerals, no Roman numerals or spelled numbers.

In the case of German units, Arabic numerals were used for divisions and small units. German corps were designated with Roman numerals such as LXXXIV Armee-Korps. Field armies were designated in the fashion 7. Armee, but army groups (Heeresgruppe) were more eccentric.

Unless otherwise noted, the photos here are from the author's collection.

GLOSSARY

ETO	European Theater of Operations
Festung	Fortress
FHO	Fremde Heer Ost: Foreign Armies East; German intelligence service for Eastern Front
GFM	Generalfeldmarschall: German field marshal
Heeresgruppe	Army group consisting of several field armies (Armee)
HKL	Hauptkampflinie: main defense line
KG	Kampfgruppe: battle group, extemporized formation a few companies to a regiment or more in size
MHI	Military History Institute, Army Historical Education Center, Carlisle Barracks, PA
NARA	National Archives and Records Administration, College Park, MD
OB West	Oberbefehlshaber West: High Command West (Rundstedt's HQ)
OKH	Oberkommando der Heeres, army high command, primarily responsible for the Eastern Front
OKW	Oberkommando der Wehrmacht: high command of the armed forces
RVK	Reichs Verteidigungs Kommissar: Reich Defense Commissars; Nazi Party officials responsible for homeland defense
SHAEF	Supreme Headquarters, Allied Expeditionary Force (Eisenhower's HQ)
Stavka	Contraction for Stavka VGK (Verkhovnogo glavnokomandovania: Staff of the Supreme High Command)
Stellung	defense line
UR	Ukreplenniy rayon: Red Army static defense sectors
Verteidigungssektor	Defense sector (in Berlin)
Wehrkreis	German military district
Zitadelle	Citadel; final defense sector in Berlin

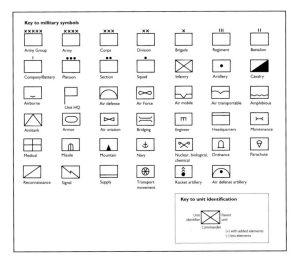

CONTENTS

The final campaign in Germany, April–May 1945

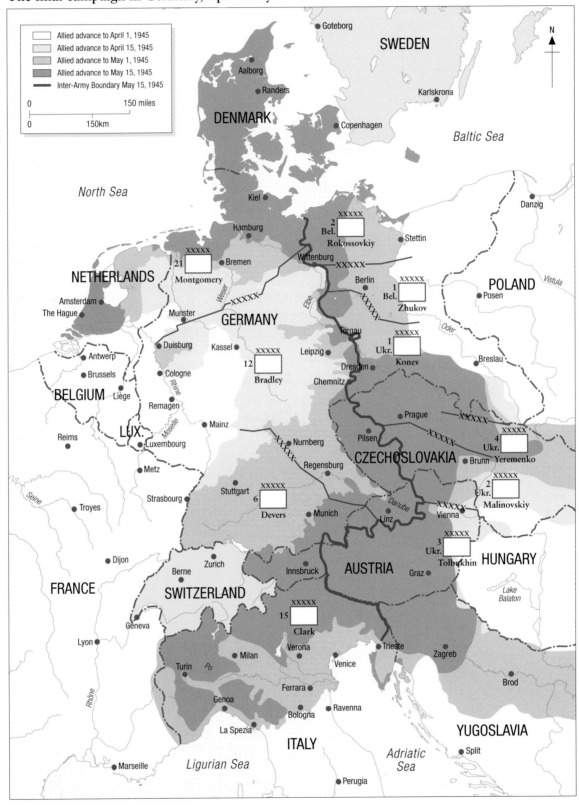

Allied advance to April 1, 1945
Allied advance to April 15, 1945
Allied advance to May 1, 1945
Allied advance to May 15, 1945
Inter-Army Boundary May 15, 1945

0   150 miles
0   150km

N

SWEDEN

Goteborg

Baltic Sea

Karlskrona

Aalborg
Randers

DENMARK

Copenhagen

North Sea

Danzig

Kiel

Hamburg

XXXXX
2
Bel.
Rokossovkiy

Stettin

POLAND

Vistula

XXXXX
21
Montgomery

Bremen

Wittenburg

XXXXX

Berlin

XXXXX
1
Bel.
Zhukov

Posen

NETHERLANDS

Weser

XXXXX

GERMANY

Elbe

Oder

Amsterdam
The Hague

Munster

Torgau

XXXXX
1
Ukr.
Konev

Breslau

Duisburg

Kassel

Leipzig

Antwerp

Cologne

XXXXX
12
Bradley

Dresden

Chemnitz

Brussels

BELGIUM   Liège

Rhine

Remagen

Prague

XXXXX

LUX.

Moselle

Mainz

XXXXX
4
Ukr.
Yeremenko

Reims

Luxembourg

Nurnberg

Pilsen

CZECHOSLOVAKIA

Brunn

XXXXX

Metz

Regensburg

XXXXX
2
Ukr.
Malinovskiy

XXXXX
6
Devers

Stuttgart

Strasbourg

Munich

Danube

XXXXX
Vienna

Linz

Seine

Troyes

XXXXX
3
Ukr.
Tolbukhin

HUNGARY

Dijon

Zurich

Berne

Innsbruck

AUSTRIA

Graz

Lake
Balaton

FRANCE

SWITZERLAND

XXXXX
15
Clark

Rhône

Geneva

Lyon

Verona

Trieste

Zagreb

Milan

Venice

Brod

Turin

Po

Ferrara

Genoa

Bologna

Ravenna

La Spezia

YUGOSLAVIA

ITALY

Adriatic
Sea

Split

Marseille

Ligurian Sea

Perugia

INTRODUCTION

By 1945, the Nazi scheme to dominate Europe had failed. It was no longer a matter of whether Germany would be defeated, but a matter of when. Hitler's sullen vindictiveness ensured that it would be a painful and bloody defeat for Germany.

In late 1944, Hitler had gambled that a strategy of holding in the east while attacking in the west would offer the best prospects of staving off the Allied onslaught. This proved to be fundamentally misguided when the Ardennes offensive was halted around Christmas 1944. At the same time, defenses against an inevitable Soviet offensive in Poland had been woefully ignored.

The Yalta conference held in Crimea in early February 1945 established the Allies' essential political and strategic conditions for ending the war. Stalin, Roosevelt, and Churchill are shown here with their foreign ministers behind them. (NARA)

On January 12, 1945, the northern tier of the Red Army launched the Vistula–Oder offensive, crushing the German defenses on the approach to Berlin. By February 1945, Soviet forces were less than 100km from Berlin. In mid-February, the Red Army shifted its focus to its southern tier along the Vienna axis and crushed the last German Panzer reserves that had launched an ill-conceived offensive around Lake Balaton in Hungary. The northern tier of the Red Army broadened its salient towards Berlin, clearing its flanks in Silesia and Pomerania before embarking on its final assault on Berlin. The violence was some of the most brutal of the entire war, engulfing not only the combatant forces but the local civilian populations as well. After years of Wehrmacht depredations in the Soviet Union, no quarter was given when the Red Army arrived on German soil.

Having repulsed the German Ardennes offensive, the Allied advance in the west resumed its grinding attritional battles along the German frontier in February 1945, preparing for an assault over the Rhine in March 1945 once the mud and rain had relented. Hitler's "stand-fast" orders trapped Heeresgruppe B in the Ruhr industrial area and its destruction by mid-April 1945 put an end to any coherent defense of western Germany. The Allied armies raced into central Germany to meet the oncoming Red Army along the Elbe River.

The final Soviet assault on Berlin began on April 14, 1945 and concluded in early May 1945. Hitler committed suicide in his command bunker in Berlin on April 30, and the military government under Admiral Dönitz brought the war to a close on May 8–9. Fighting continued for more than a week including a major campaign around Prague. This book focuses on the central fronts in Germany during the final month of the war in April–May 1945.

Ambiguities in the Yalta accords over the fate of Austria encouraged Stalin to switch the focus of the March and early April fighting from the Berlin axis to the Vienna axis. Here, a battery of SU-76M assault guns of the 3rd Ukrainian Front support an infantry attack in Austria in April 1945.

CHRONOLOGY

January 12	Red Army launches Vistula–Oder offensive.
February 4	Stalin, Roosevelt, and Churchill meet at Yalta in the Crimea to discuss the conclusion of the war.
February 8	British 21st Army Group launches Operation *Veritable* to break through the Reichswald.
February 8	Ninth US Army launches Operation *Grenade* to seize the Roer dams.
February 15	Wehrmacht launches Operation *Sonnenwende* trying to stymie the Red Army advance on Berlin.
February 17	Stalin halts the drive on Berlin in favor of eliminating the threat to the flanks and pushing on towards Vienna.
February 22	Northern tier of the Red Army launches offensive in Pomerania to pre-empt any future threat from the northern flank.
March 6	Wehrmacht launches Operation *Frühlingserwachen* in Hungary, the last major German offensive of the war.
March 7	US 9th Armored Division unexpectedly captures the Rhine bridge at Remagen.
March 16	Southern tier of Soviet armies begins its offensive towards Vienna.
March 22–23	Patton's Third US Army crosses the Rhine at Oppenheim.
March 22–23	Red Army surrounds Festung Küstrin and seizes a bridgehead over the Oder.
March 24	21st Army Group stages Operation *Plunder–Veritable* to cross the Rhine near Wesel.
March 24	Ninth US Army launches Operation *Flashpoint* to cross the Rhine north of the Ruhr pocket.
March 25	First US Army launches Operation *Voyage*, the break-out from the Remagen bridgehead.
April 1	First US Army and Ninth US Army meet at Lippstadt, encircling Heeresgruppe B in the Ruhr pocket.
April 11	US 2nd Armored Division reaches the Elbe River.
April 12	The 1st Belorussian Front begins the preliminary bombardment for a new offensive.

April 15	Vienna falls to the Red Army.
April 15	15. Armee in the Ruhr surrenders.
April 16	Red Army Berlin operation begins.
April 18	Ruhr pocket collapses.
April 20	Red Army spearheads reach the outskirts of Berlin.
April 20	2nd Belorussian Front begins offensive into northern Germany.
April 21	OKW headquarters at Zossen captured by Soviet tanks.
April 23	11. Armee in Festung Harz surrenders.
April 25	Red Army completes encirclement of Berlin.
April 25	American and Soviet forces meet on the Elbe near Torgau.
April 29	21st Army Group launches Operation *Enterprise* to reach the Baltic ahead of the Red Army.
April 30	Hitler commits suicide in his bunker near the Reich Chancellery.
May 2	Berlin ceasefire begins at 1500hrs.
May 4	Salzburg falls to the Seventh US Army.
May 4	Germans sign ceasefire at Montgomery's HQ covering northern Germany.
May 5	Czech resistance forces stage Prague uprising.
May 7	At 0241hrs, Jodl signs the instrument of surrender at Reims.
May 8–9	War ends at midnight.
May 9	At 0016hrs, second surrender ceremony at Zhukov's headquarters in Berlin.
May 11	Most fighting in Prague ends.
May 15	Ceasefire in Yugoslavia.

THE STRATEGIC SITUATION

In light of Germany's declining military resources in the final months of 1944, Hitler decided on a policy of "Attack in the West – Defend in the East." Germany's limited reserves were directed to Heeresgruppe B (Army Group B) for the Ardennes offensive. Reinforcements to the east were limited to a trickle. The Ardennes offensive quickly failed when its *Schwerpunkt* (focal point), the 1. SS-Panzer-Korps attack in the northern sector, failed to make an operational penetration of the American defenses in the first week of the attack. The neighboring 5. Panzer-Armee did succeed in making a penetration beyond Bastogne by Christmas, but this success along a secondary axis held no prospect for redeeming the offensive. When the 5. Panzer-Armee advance was crushed in the days after Christmas, the Ardennes campaign turned into an attritional struggle which Germany had no chance of winning. Instead of shifting Germany's meager Panzer resources east to confront an inevitable Soviet winter offensive, Hitler dithered and left them in the west to pursue the paltry objective of capturing Bastogne.

In the east, the Fremde Heer Ost intelligence service issued dire warnings about the prospect for a major Soviet winter offensive from their bridgeheads on the west bank of the Vistula River in central Poland. The FHO estimated that the Red Army enjoyed more than a 3:1 advantage, which Hitler dismissed

A tank column from the 1st Mechanized Corps of the 3rd Ukrainian Front advances through the streets of Vienna on April 11, 1945. The tanks are Lend-Lease M4A2 medium tanks while the truck is a captured Hungarian 38M Raba Botond.

German troops inspect a T-34-85 of the 222nd Separate Tank Regiment, knocked out during the street fighting in Breslau on March 7, 1945 while supporting the attacks of the 52nd Army of the 1st Ukrainian Front. The Red Army bypassed the Silesian city during the Oder offensive of January 1945, and Festung Breslau remained under siege until after the capitulation was signed in May 1945. This tank regiment subsequently was decorated with the Order of Bogdan Khemilnitskiy 2nd Class for its combat actions in the siege of Breslau, now Wrocław, Poland.

as a gross exaggeration. In fact, the Soviet deception plan had led the FHO to underestimate the actual Red Army strength in Poland, which was 5:1 overall. The Soviet Vistula–Oder offensive was launched on January 12, 1945 and quickly shattered the German defenses. Four Soviet fronts pushed some 700km towards Germany, smashing Heeresgruppe Mitte (Army Group Center) and Heeresgruppe A. The two main Soviet fronts pushed through western Poland and by late January reached the Oder River near the fortress city of Küstrin, only 100km from Berlin. On the Baltic, the Red Army's 3rd Belorussian Front struck into Prussia, aiming for the provincial capital of Königsberg. By early February, a substantial German force was trapped along the Baltic coast from Danzig to the Kurland peninsula in Latvia.

The cataclysmic defeat of two army groups in late January 1945 forced Hitler to reorient his defensive strategy to favor the reinforcement of the east over the west. This is very evident when looking at the allotment of critical equipment such as tanks and armored fighting vehicles (AFVs) as detailed in the accompanying chart. In addition, Berlin belatedly began to reallocate its most powerful mobile forces. The 6. SS-Panzer-Armee was pulled out of the Ardennes in mid-January 1945 and reassigned to the Eastern Front. A new army group, Heeresgruppe Weichsel (Army Group Vistula) was created under the command of Heinrich Himmler to defend the approaches to Berlin.

The 2nd and 3rd Belorussian Fronts continued to clear the northern flanks along the Baltic in March and April 1945. This is a Kingtiger tank of s.Pz.Abt. 505, one of the last two of the battalion during the final fighting near Fischhausen near Pillau during the Soviet campaign to clear the East Prussian capital of Königsberg in April 1945. (Viktor Kulikov)

Paratroopers of the US 17th Airborne Division ride aboard a British Churchill tank of the Guards Armoured Brigade on March 24 during the fighting near Appelhulsen during Operation *Varsity–Plunder*, the crossing of the Rhine by Montgomery's 21st Army Group. (NARA)

Delivery of German AFVs by theater

	November 1944	December 1944	January 1945	February 1945	March 1945
West	1,345	952	343	67	134
East	288	631	1,264	1,455	367
Total	1,633	1,583	1,607	1,522	501

On February 4, 1945, Stalin, Roosevelt, and Churchill met in Yalta to discuss the final endgame against Germany. The meeting reaffirmed the policy of unconditional surrender, and established boundaries where the advancing armies were expected to meet. The German capital of Berlin was inside the Soviet zone.

Until the Yalta conference, Soviet front commanders had anticipated that the January Vistula–Oder offensive would continue to the gates of Berlin. Marshal Georgi Zhukov had outlined plans in late January for the next phase of the Berlin operation, which he presumed would be concluded by the end of February. Instead, Stalin ordered an abrupt change of focus on February 17. This was prompted in part by the tactical situation as well as by the political ramifications of the Yalta conference. Stalin had noted that the occupation of Austria had not been resolved at Yalta, and he saw a political opportunity to extend Soviet control to Vienna and the Danube basin. From a military standpoint, Stalin was worried that a rash lunge for Berlin might result in a catastrophe as had occurred to the Russian Army at the gates of Berlin in 1760, and the Red Army at Warsaw in 1920. The two Soviet fronts nearest to Berlin still had substantial German forces on their flanks, especially a large concentration of forces on

A Churchill Crocodile flamethrower tank of the British 79th Armoured Division passes in front of a church in Sterkrade, Germany on March 31, 1945 following Operation *Plunder*. The plume of smoke in the background is from a massive fire at a nearby synthetic fuel plant. (NARA)

the northern flank in Prussia and Pomerania. Hitler's decision to commit his last reserve, the 6. SS-Panzer-Armee, to the Budapest sector was further evidence of German intentions to threaten the Soviet advance from its flanks.

As a result of these factors, Stalin ordered that the northern tier of fronts deal with the Pomeranian and Prussian flanks, while at the same time, the southern tier was instructed to crush German and Hungarian resistance around Budapest, and to move westward to Austria. The fronts facing Berlin would be reinforced, but the final assault on Berlin would wait. Stalin was well aware that the western Allies were still recovering from the Ardennes and Nordwind offensives, and were not expected to resume their offensives until March. This gave the Red Army plenty of time to conduct its new missions prior to the final assault on Berlin.

In mid-February, the Germans launched Operation *Sonnenwende* (*Solstice*) that was intended to cut off the Red Army's spearhead, the 2nd Guards Tank Army, on the Oder near Küstrin. Given the catastrophic losses suffered in January 1945 and the paucity of resources, *Sonnenwende* had little impact and merely served to weaken German forces in Pomerania on the eve of the Red Army offensive to clear out the Baltic coast. The Red Army launched the Pomeranian offensive on February 22 that lasted for three weeks. The offensive crushed the German forces all the way to the Baltic coast, even though a few German cities such as Kolberg and Danzig remained surrounded and defiant. By the end of February, the Wehrmacht in the east had suffered massive losses, with casualties totaling 606,000 in January–February, including 77,000 dead and 195,000 missing.

Patton's Third US Army crossed the Rhine near Oppenheim and quickly shattered the defenses of Heeresgruppe G. Here, a column of M4A3E8 tanks of the 6th Armored Division drive down the autobahn on March 29, 1945 while vast columns of German POWs stream to the rear. (NARA)

The fighting around Budapest since December 1944 had turned into a costly attritional struggle on both sides. The Red Army had seized the eastern side of Budapest by January 18, and the surviving German garrison on the western bank of the Danube withdrew on February 12. Hitler remained obsessed with the Danube axis, and, in early March, ordered Heeresgruppe Süd to launch Operation *Frühlingserwachen* (*Spring Awakening*), consisting of the 6. Armee and the 6. SS-Panzer-Armee. This pincer attack in the Lake Balaton area was intended to cut off the 3rd Ukrainian Front. Soviet intelligence was aware of the plans, and Moscow ordered the 3rd Ukrainian Front to hunker down and repel the attack without dipping into the reserves being built up for the Vienna operation later in the month. The last major German offensive of the war started on March 6 and lasted a little more than a week before it ran out of steam. Four Soviet armies secreted themselves on the left flank of the German attack and launched their counterattack on March 16. The 2nd and 3rd Ukrainian fronts unleashed the Vienna offensive and penetrated deep into the threadbare German lines. German defenses in the eastern Danube collapsed and the 6th Guards Tank Army reached Vienna on April 13, 1945. With both the northern and southern flanks secure, the Red Army was ready for its final assault on Berlin.

In the west, the Rhine River was the last substantial geographic barrier to Allied entry into Germany's industrial heartland in the Ruhr and the Saar. On February 8, Montgomery's 21st Army Group launched Operation *Veritable* to break through the Reichswald to the Rhine while the Ninth US Army launched Operation *Grenade* to seize the Roer dams. Bradley's 12th Army Group conducted Operation *Lumberjack* to clear the western bank of the Rhine in their sector. During this operation, the 9th Armored Division unexpectedly captured the Ludendorff Bridge over the Rhine at Remagen on March 7, giving the Allies a small foothold on the eastern bank. The Remagen bridgehead changed Eisenhower's plans. Instead of a sole focus on Montgomery's Rhine crossing, Operation *Varsity–Plunder*, Eisenhower authorized a broader scheme to push over the Rhine at multiple points. Patton's Third US Army crossed the Rhine at Oppenheim on the night of March 22–23, and Montgomery's British–Canadian armies crossed on schedule near Wesel on March 24.

The Seventh US Army began crossing the Rhine south of Worms on March 26 using boats and rafts. This is a squad from the 7th Infantry, 3rd Infantry Division disembarking near Frankenthal. (NARA)

OPPOSING COMMANDERS

GERMAN COMMANDERS

Adolf Hitler served as the supreme military authority in Germany, and after the failed military coup on July 20, 1944, he took an ever more intrusive role in military planning. The German military command structure included two supreme commands, the OKW (Oberkommando der Wehrmacht), nominally the high command of the armed forces, and the OKH (Oberkommando der Heeres), nominally the army high command. In practice, the OKH tended to be responsible for the Eastern Front while the OKW managed the armed forces overall and also directed the Western Front and scattered theaters such as Norway, Italy, and the Balkans. The OKW was led by **GFM (Generalfeldmarschall) Wilhelm Keitel** who held the post from the start of the war and was widely regarded as a servile creature of Hitler. The OKH had been led by **Generaloberst Heinz Guderian** following the July 20 coup. He was respected by Hitler, but they had a testy relationship in late 1944–early 1945 due to Guderian's insistence that more attention be paid to the Eastern Front. He was relieved of command on March 28, 1945 and replaced by **General der Infanterie Hans Krebs**.

Hitler's last trip to the front was this visit to the command post of Cl. Armee-Korps at Schloss Harnekop on the Oder Front on March 3, 1945. The corps commander, Gen.Lt. Friedrich Sixt, can be seen at the extreme right. (Library of Congress)

There were four theater commands in 1945, the Oberost command having been abolished in July 1940 and the role taken over by OKH. The most important of these was OB West (Oberbefehlshaber West), headed off-and-on by **GFM Gerd von Rundstedt** since October 1940. Rundstedt was widely regarded as Germany's finest senior commander, but he periodically ran afoul of Hitler and was sacked for the last time on March 10, 1945 due to the Remagen debacle. **Generalfeldmarschall Albert Kesselring,** the former OB Südwest commander, took his place. Kesselring was a Luftwaffe commander best known for his leadership of German forces in the Mediterranean theater including North Africa since January 1942. Oberbefehlshaber Südost covered the Balkans and was led for much of the war by **GFM Maximilian Freiherr von Weichs,** replaced by Luftwaffe **Generaloberst Alexander Löhr** on March 21, 1945.

ABOVE LEFT
Generalfeldmarschall Walter Model commanded Heeresgruppe B at the time of the Ruhr encirclement. He is seen here on the left in the late summer of 1944 talking with Gen. der Panzertruppe Gerhard Graf von Schwerin at the 116. Panzer-Division headquarters. (MHI)

ABOVE RIGHT
Generalfeldmarschall Albert Kesselring was most closely associated with his commands in the Mediterranean in 1943–44 and he is seen here visiting a *Fallschirmjäger* command post in northern Italy on February 16, 1945. In March 1945, he was assigned to take over the OB West command from Rundstedt, and he later took over the entire southern theater after German forces were bifurcated by the Allied offensives in late April 1945. (Library of Congress)

After the July 1944 military coup attempt against Hitler, SS chief Heinrich Himmler increasingly attempted to insert himself into army affairs, taking over the Replacement Army, and then taking over field army commands in Alsace in 1944 and on the Oder Front in early 1945. Here he is seen awarding the Close-Combat Medal in Gold to army and Waffen-SS soldiers in December 1944. (Library of Congress)

The army had several army groups (*Heeresgruppen*) in 1945, but this discussion is confined to the most central. Under OB West in the west, Heeresgruppe B was the principal command deployed from the Dutch frontier to the Saar; it was commanded in 1945 by **GFM Walter Model**. To its north was Heeresgruppe H, commanded in early 1945 by **Generaloberst Johannes Blaskowitz**. The area from the Saar to the Swiss frontier was managed by Heeresgruppe G, led by **Oberstgruppenführer-SS Paul Hausser** though April 4, 1945 when command was transferred to **Gen. der. Inf. Friedrich Schulz**.

The OKH controlled four army groups at the start of the 1945 campaigns. Heeresgruppe Nord became trapped in the Kurland peninsula and underwent several name changes and command changes as its perimeter shrank. At the start of the Soviet Vistula–Oder offensive, Heeresgruppe Mitte (Center) was

the primary formation from the Baltic to the Danube and was commanded by **Generaloberst Georg-Hans Reinhardt**. It was destroyed by the offensive and so Hitler created the new Heeresgruppe Weichsel (Vistula) under the command of **SS-Reichsführer Heinrich Himmler**. He had previously commanded the Heeresgruppe Oberrhein (Upper Rhine) in Alsace during the Operation *Nordwind* offensive in early January 1945. He had no military experience at all and one German commander described his military understanding as "childish." He proved to be a source of endless aggravation for the army commanders and many of the military directives for HG Weichsel were in fact issued by Guderian. Heeresgruppe A, which had been covering the Silesian front at the start of the offensive, was crushed in the attack; the remnants were put under the command of **GFM Ferdinand Schörner** and it was renamed Heeresgruppe Mitte. It covered the Czech lands and Austria. Heeresgruppe Süd covered the Danube basin and was commanded by **Gen. der Inf. Friedrich Schulz** from April 2, 1945.

SOVIET COMMANDERS

The Soviet dictator **Iosef V. Stalin** held ultimate control over the Red Army, leading the Stavka VGK (Verkhovnogo glavnokomandovania: Staff of the Supreme High Command); **Gen. Boris Shapshnikov** directed the headquarters on a day-to-day basis. The senior Red Army leaders were the front commanders; Soviet fronts were roughly the equivalent of German *Heeresgruppen* or Anglo-American army groups. Stalin shifted his best commanders from front to front and in April 1945 had his three best, Zhukov, Rokossovskiy, and Konev, on the central fronts facing Berlin.

The commander of the 1st Belorussian Front was the Soviet Union's most celebrated commander, **Marshal Georgi K. Zhukov**, 46 years old in 1945. He was a cavalry squadron commander in the Russian Civil War, and in 1939 he commanded the Soviet forces in Mongolia. This brought him to Stalin's attention when his forces defeated the Japanese at the battle for Khalkin Gol in 1939. At the start of the war, he was head of the General Staff. Stalin regarded him as his most able general, and he rotated between senior leadership positions with the Stavka in Moscow to field commands in critical sectors. He took command of the 1st Belorussian Front in November 1944 in preparation for the Vistula–Oder offensive.

Marshal Georgi Konstantinovich Zhukov was "the first among equals" of the front commanders, selected by Stalin in November 1944 to lead the 1st Belorussian Front on the most direct path to Berlin. (NARA)

The commander of the 1st Ukrainian Front was **Marshal Ivan S. Konev,** 48 years old in 1945. He had served as a political commissar in the Russian Civil War and had escaped the purges as a commander in the remote Baikal and Caucasus military districts. He was at the center of many of the great battles on the Eastern Front including Smolensk and Moscow in 1941, the Kursk and Dnepr campaigns in 1943, the battles in Ukraine in early 1944, and the forcing of the Vistula River during Operation *Bagration* in the summer of 1944.

The commander of the 2nd Belorussian Front was **Marshal Konstantin K. Rokossovskiy,** 49 years old in 1945. He led a cavalry regiment in the Civil War in 1918–20. Of Polish origins, he fell under suspicion during the Great Purge and was imprisoned, but rehabilitated in 1940. He was one of the Soviet Union's most talented senior commanders, and led a succession of major commands including the Briansk Front in July 1942, the Don Front in September 1942 during the Stalingrad battles, and the Central Front in February–October 1943 during the Kursk campaign. He led the 1st Belorussian Front from February 1944 but was transferred to the 2nd Belorussian Front in November 1944 to give Zhukov command of the main front aimed at Berlin.

WESTERN ALLIED COMMANDERS

Of the two principal Allied political leaders, **Winston Churchill** took the more active role in military affairs; **Franklin Roosevelt** deferred to the US Army chief-of-staff, **Gen. George C. Marshall.** The strategy of the Allied forces was coordinated through a Combined Chiefs of Staff (CCS) and Churchill's influence was largely through the power of persuasion, and not through direct control as in the case of the Soviet and German dictators.

General Dwight Eisenhower led SHAEF (Supreme Headquarters Allied Expeditionary Force), which roughly corresponded to Rundstedt's OB West command. He had three army groups under his command. **Field Marshal**

Bernard L. Montgomery led the 21st Army Group, consisting of the Canadian First Army and British Second Army. Montgomery led the Allied ground forces in Normandy through August 1944 when the US field armies under Bradley formed an independent command. At various points in 1944 and 1945, he pressed Eisenhower to promote him to land forces commander over the three Allied army groups. Eisenhower resisted this initiative, in no small measure due to Montgomery's difficult personality and his troubles working with the senior American commanders. **General Omar Bradley's** 12th Army Group was the largest of the Allied formations, consisting of four American field armies in April 1945. He was a close confidant of Eisenhower, and part of a coterie from the 1942–43 Mediterranean campaign who Eisenhower

The senior Allied commanders in the northern tier at the time of the Operation *Varsity–Plunder* Rhine crossing. From left to right are Lt. Gen. Miles C. Dempsey (British Second Army), Lt. Gen. Courtney Hodges (First US Army), Field Marshal Bernard L. Montgomery (21st Army Group), Lt. Gen. William Simpson (Ninth US Army), and Lt. Gen. Harry D. G. Crerar (First Canadian Army). (NARA)

favored. The southern tier was the 6th Army Group, commanded by **Gen. Jacob Devers** that included the Seventh US Army and the 1ere Armée Française (French First Army). As Eisenhower's only real rival for senior command, Devers' relations with SHAEF were strained. Eisenhower kept Devers' command small even as Bradley's command accrued more and more field armies. Command of the 6th Army Group was all the more difficult since it contained **Gen. Jean de Lattre de Tassigny's** French army. De Lattre generally followed Devers' instructions, but there were a number of occasions where he received direct commands from the French leader **Gen. Charles de Gaulle** dealing with matters of French sovereignty that interfered with Devers' orders.

OPPOSING ARMIES

THE GERMAN ARMY

The decline in German military power at the end of 1944 had been brought about by repeated battlefield defeats as well as the destruction of German military industry by the Combined Bomber Offensive. The loss of Romania's oil fields in August 1944 and the Allied bombing attacks on Germany's synthetic fuel plants was drying up the Wehrmacht's fuel supply and so crippling its tactical mobility. Furthermore, fuel shortages led to debilitating cutbacks in the training of tank and aircraft crews. While the Wehrmacht had often been able to maintain tactical parity in spite of numerical inferiority to its opponents, the decline in training robbed it of its tactical edge.

By the beginning of 1945, there was a noticeable decrease in the supply of critical weapons and munitions, and the decline accelerated in 1945 due to Allied bombing attacks against both the factories and the railroad network supporting them. German industry was in a precipitous decline by the end of 1944 due to the synergistic effects of the Allied bombing campaign, which had shifted its focus against the German industry's transportation network.

Manpower shortages led to the induction of younger and younger age groups into the army in 1945. Here, some teenagers from the Hitlerjugend have been attached to a Volkssturm unit in a town in Pomerania on the Oder Front on February 28, 1945 and are receiving instruction. The soldier was an experienced combat veteran judging from his Iron Cross.

Aside from growing shortages of fuel and critical materials, the destruction of the rail network, especially in western Germany, prevented the shipment of coal to industry with resulting collapses in steel and chemical production. By the end of February 1945, the defense industries had essentially collapsed.

German tank and AFV operational strength, April 10, 1945

	East	West	Other*	Total**
Total	2,173	226	963	3,362

*Includes Südost, Südwest, Norway, Denmark

**Actual strength was 4,933 including tanks in repair and battle-damaged tanks

The disastrous summer battles of 1944 cut into the German order of battle. At the start of 1945, the Wehrmacht, including Waffen-SS and Luftwaffe ground units, totaled 238 infantry divisions and 51 Panzer/Panzergrenadier divisions, a decline of 25 divisions since the beginning of 1944. Of these surviving divisions, 169 were facing the Red Army and 120 were in the west or in other theaters such as Norway. Aside from the loss of German strength, allied strength collapsed with the defection of Romania, Finland, Bulgaria, and Slovakia. Hungary and the rump Italian RSI state remained the sole significant German allies.

German divisional strength, east and west, 1945

	January 21	January 26	February 1	March 31	April 12	April 30
HG Kurland		26	26	20	20	
HG Nord*	29	36	32	46	26	
HG Weichsel		13	19	25	23	
HG Mitte	44	38	35	47	45	60
HG A	37					
HG Süd	26	24	24	37	36	29
OKH Subtotal	136	137	140	175	163	89
Norway	12	12	12	10	10	
OB West	73	73	68	58	65	25
OB Südwest	24	24	23	22	19	21
OB Südost	9	9	9	7	8	10
OKW Subtotal	118	118	113	99	112	56
Total**	254+26	255+24	253+28	274+22	275+22	145+3

* Heeresgruppe Nord reduced to AOK Ostpreussen in April 1945

**Total includes: (deployed divisions) +(replacement and security divisions and divisions being rebuilt)

The exceptionally heavy casualties suffered in 1944 created serious manpower shortages in the German Army. Overall strength of the armed forces fell from about 9.4 million in 1944 to about 7.8 million at the start of 1945. Total casualties in 1944 were 2.9 million including 345,600 dead, 1,174,000 missing and 1,382,000 wounded, with the losses falling most heavily on the army. This led to a variety of expedients, including the reduction in the age of conscription to 16. The German Army came to depend increasingly on large-scale fortification programs to serve as a crutch for the infantry. These defense programs, the West Stellung and Ost Stellung, employed tens of thousands of civilians and forced laborers to create earthen entrenchments, tank traps, and other field fortifications.

The most desperate action was the creation of the Volkssturm, a militia based on underage boys and overage men. The Volkssturm was formed under Nazi Party control in September–October 1944, over the objections of the army, which felt that a poorly trained militia would have little combat value. Volkssturm units proved to be largely ineffective in the west where local communities had no interest in seeing their towns destroyed in futile gestures of defiance, but the Volkssturm did have some tactical impact in eastern Germany where the fear of Soviet atrocities stiffened the resolve of the local German defenses.

German Army casualties 1945

	Jan	Feb	Mar	Apr*	Subtotal
Russian Front	73,025	316,553	343,127	194,276	926,981
Balkan Front	3,212	10,217	10,904	4,752	29,085
Western Front	65,429	74,294	56,638	272,363	468,724
Italian Front	4,751	4,232	7,982	11,131	28,096
Total	146,417	405,296	418,651	482,522	1,452,886
Killed	21,898	55,422	51,402	22,537	151,259
Wounded	87,904	247,899	220,398	94,753	650,954
Missing	36,615	101,975	146,851	365,232	650,673

*April data includes only first two weeks

BELOW RIGHT
Germany's large cities were defended by thick belts of heavy Flak guns to protect against Allied bomber attack. During the 1945 ground campaigns, they often formed the core of German defense lines. This 128mm Flak 40 was deployed with the 14. Flak-Division defending the Leuna refinery, east of Leipzig on the approaches to the Elbe. This division claimed the destruction of 147 American tanks during the fighting in this sector in April 1945, mainly fighting the US 2nd Armored Division. (NARA)

GERMAN ARMY ORDER OF BATTLE, APRIL 12, 1945

WEHRMACHT IN THE EAST

OKH (Oberkommando des Heeres)	Gen. der Inf. Hans Krebs
Heeresgruppe Kurland	**Gen. Carl Hilpert**
16. Armee	Gen. der Geb. Friedrich Volckamer von Kirchensittenbeach
XVI. Armee-Korps	Gen.Lt. Gottfried Weber
VI. SS-Korps	Obergruppenführer Walther Krüger
XXXVIII. Panzer-Korps	Gen. der Pz. Maximilian Reichsfreiherr von Edelsheim
18. Armee	Gen. der Inf. Ehrenfried Boege
L. Armee-Korps	Gen.Lt. Erpo Frieherr von Bodenhausen
II. Armee-Korps	Gen. Lt. Alfred Gause
I. Armee-Korps	Gen. der Inf. Friedrich Fangohr
X. Armee-Korps	Gen. der Art. Siegfried Thomaschiki
AOK Ost Preussen	**Gen. Alfred Gause**
VI. Korps	Gen. der Inf. Horst Grossmann
Kdt. Pillau	Gen. Lt. Kurt Chill
IX. Armee-Korps	Gen. Lt. Hermann Hohn
XXVI. Armee-Korps	Gen. der Inf. Gerhard Matzky
XVIII. Gebirgs-Korps	Gen. der Geb. Friedrich Hochbaum
XXIII. Armee-Korps	Gen. der Inf. Walter Melzer
Gen.Kdo.Hela	Gen. der Inf. Karl-Wilhem Specht
Heeresgruppe Weichsel	**Gen. Gotthard Heinrici**
3. Panzer-Armee	Gen. Hasso von Manteuffel
XXXII. Armee-Korps	Gen. der Inf. Friedrich Schack
XXVII. Armee-Korps (Oder-Korps)	Gen.Lt. Wolf Hagemann
XXXXVI. Panzer-Korps	Gen. der Inf. Martin Gareis
9. Armee	Gen. der Inf. Theodor Busse
CI. Armee-Korps	Gen.Lt. Friedrich Sixt
LVI. Panzer-Korps	Gen. der Art. Helmuth Weidling
XI. SS-Panzer-Korps	SS-Obergruppenführer Mathias Kleinheisterkamp
V. SS-Gebirgs-Korps	Gen. der WSS Jaeckel
Heeresgruppe Mitte	**GFM Ferdinand Schörner**
4. Panzer-Armee	Gen. Fritz-Herbert Gräser
V. Armee-Korps	Gen. der Art. Wägner
Panzer-Korps "Grossdeutschland"	Gen. der Panzertruppe Georg Jauer
LVII. Panzer-Korps	Gen. der Pz. Friedrich Kirchner
17. Armee	Gen. der Inf. Wilhelm Hasse
VIII. Armee-Korps	Gen. der Art. Horts von Mellenthin
XVII. Armee-Korps	Gen. der Pio. Otto Tiemann
XXXX. Panzer-Korps	Gen. der Pz. Siegfried Henrici
1. Panzer-Armee	Gen. der Pz. Walther Nehring
XXIV. Panzer-Korps	Gen.Lt. Hans Källner
XI. Armee-Korps	Gen. der Inf. Rudolf Bünau
LIX. Armee-Korps	Gen.Lt. Ernst Sieler
XXXXIX. Gebirgs-Korps	Gen. der Geb. Karl von Le Suire
XXIX. Armee-Korps	Gen. der Inf. Kurt Röpke
Heeresgruppe Süd	**General der Inf. Friedrich Schulz**
8. Armee	Gen. der Geb. Hans Kreysing
LXXII. Armee-Korps	Gen. der Inf. Anton Dostler
IV. Panzer-Korps "Feldherrnhalle"	Gen. der Pz. Ulrich Kleeman
XXXXIII. Armee-Korps	Gen. der Geb. Kurt Versock
6. SS-Panzer-Armee	Oberstgruppenführer Sepp Dietrich
II. SS-Panzer-Korps	Obergruppenführer Willi Bittrich
III. Panzer-Korps	Gen. der Pz. Hermann Breith
IV. SS-Panzer-Korps	Obergruppenführer Herbert Gille
2. Panzer-Armee	Gen. der Art. Maximilian de Angelis
I. Kav.-Korps	Gen. der Kav. Gustav Harteneck
XXII. Gebirgs-Korps	Gen. der Geb. Hubert Lanz
LXVIII. Armee-Korps	Gen. der Geb. Rudolf Konrad
LVI. Panzer-Korps	Gen. der Art. Helmuth Weidling

WEHRMACHT IN THE WEST

OKW (Oberkommando der Wehrmacht)	**GFM Wilhelm Keitel**
OB Nordwest	**GFM Ernst Busch**
XXX. Armee-Korps	Gen. der Kav. Philipp Kleffel
LXXXVIII. Armee-Korps	Gen. der Inf. Eugen Schwalbe
1. Fallschirmjäger-Armee	Gen. Kurt Student
II. Fallschirmjäger-Korps	Gen.Lt. Alfred Gause
LXXXVI. Armee-Korps	Gen. der Inf. Erich Straube
Heeresgruppe B	**GFM Walter Model**
Armee Abteilung von Lüttwitz	Gen. Heinrich Freiherr von Lüttwitz
LIII. Armee-Korps	Gen.Lt. Fritz Beyerlein
LXIII. Armee-Korps	Gen. der Inf. Erich Abraham
5. Panzer-Armee	Gen. Josef Harpe
XII. SS-Korps	Gen.Lt. Eduard Crasemann
LVIII. Panzer-Korps	Gen. der Pz. Friedrich Kirchner
15. Armee	Gen. der Inf. Gustav von Zangen
LXXIV. Armee-Korps	Gen. der Inf. Carl Püchler
LXXXI. Armee-Korps	Gen.Lt. Ernst-Günther Baade
11. Armee	Gen. der Art. Walther Lucht
LXVI. Armee-Korps	Gen. Lt. Hermann Flörke
IX. Armee-Korps	Gen. der Art. Rolf Wuthmann
LXVII. Armee-Korps	Gen. der Inf. Otto Hitzfeld
OB West	**GFM Albert Kesselring**
7. Armee	Gen. der Inf. Hans von Obstfelder
LXXX. Armee-Korps	Gen. der Fli. Erich Petersen

LXXXV. Armee-Korps	Gen. der Pz. Smilo Freiherr von Lüttwitz	LXXX. Armee-Korps	Gen. der Art. Hermann Tittel
XII. Armee-Korps	Gen. der Art. Herbert Osterkamp	LXIV. Armee-Korps	Gen.Lt. Helmut Friebe
LXXXII. Armee-Korps	Gen.Lt. Theodor Tolsdorff	XVIII. AS-Korps	Gruppenführer Georg Keppler
1. Armee	Gen. der Kav. Rudolf Koch-Erpach	Marine Oberkommando West	Admiral Theodor Krancke
XIII. SS-Korps	Gruppenführer Max Simon	XXV. Armee-Korps	Gen. der Inf. Hans von Obstfelder
XIII. Armee-Korps	Gen.Lt. Max Bork		
19. Armee	Gen. der Pz. Erik Brandenberger		

THE RED ARMY

The Red Army in the spring of 1945 deployed about 6.1 million troops in its fronts and independent armies out of a total strength of about 10.2 million in uniform. This was actually a decline from its peak deployed strength of 6.7 million in the last quarter of 1944. The manpower shortages were due to heavy wartime losses combined with the deportation of large numbers of Soviet citizens to Germany for forced labor, which by 1945 totaled 5.3 million people. The peak year of military conscription was 1943 with nearly two million recruits; this fell to 1.3 million in 1944. As a result of these shortages, the Red Army was one of the few to make extensive use of women in combat roles. At the start of 1945, there were nearly a half-million women in the Red Army.

As a result of the personnel shortages, the Red Army force structure in the spring of 1945 was somewhat smaller than at its peak. For example, the peak strength of rifle divisions was reached in late 1944 at around 470 divisions while this had contracted to about 460 rifle divisions by April–May 1945.

It should be kept in mind that Soviet divisions were usually at much lower strengths than their tables of organization would suggest, and comparisons between Allied armies based on the number of divisions can be very misleading. For example, the nominal strength of a Soviet rifle division under the December 1944 tables was 11,706 troops. At the start of the advance on Berlin in April 1945, the Guards rifle divisions of Chuikov's 8th Guards, the

The mobility of the Red Army in 1945 was substantially enhanced by the provision of large quantities of Lend-Lease trucks. One of the most popular was the Studebaker US-6 2.5 ton truck. The truck in the background is a ZiS-5V, a license-built Soviet copy of an early 1930s US commercial truck.

The Red Army made more extensive use of "Katyusha" multiple rocket launchers for artillery missions than most armies of the period. This is a BM-13N, the most common version in 1945, consisting of 16 rails for 132mm rockets on a Lend-Lease Studebaker US-6 truck. This example is currently preserved at the Victory Museum at Poklonna Gora on the outskirts of Moscow.

focal point of the Soviet offensive, had on average only 4,990 men, less than half their authorized strength. As a result, most Soviet rifle corps were closer in strength to British or American infantry divisions. Likewise, field armies were much smaller than their Anglo-American counterparts.

In spite of the modest decline in force structure by 1945, the combat power of the Red Army steadily increased due to greater tactical prowess brought about by combat experience, more thorough training, and better equipment. One indicator of the shifting effectiveness was the exchange ratio in personnel casualties between Soviet and Axis forces during the conflict. In the opening phase of the war, June 22, 1941 to Stalingrad in November 1942, the Red Army was suffering 3.2 casualties for every enemy loss. By the middle of the war, the ratio had declined to 2.7 to 1, and in 1944–45, it dropped to 1.4 to 1.

There was a significant increase in armored vehicle strength from 1944 to 1945, going from about 24,400 tanks and AFVs in January 1944 to 35,400 in January 1945. Not only had the Soviet tank and AFV inventory increased, but there had been important improvements in quality. Firepower also substantially improved. Soviet field artillery totaled 53,100 guns and howitzers at the beginning of 1944, and rose to 62,300 at the beginning of 1945.

The Red Army had become very proficient in river-crossing operations by 1945, even though its technical means were not as sophisticated as those of Britain and the United States. This truck column is carrying bridge pontoons on ZiS-5 trucks.

Red Army order of battle, deployed forces, May 1, 1945*

Fronts	Commander	Armies	Air Armies	Rifle div.	Cav. div.	Art. corps	Art. div.	Tank corps	Mech. corps
Leningrad Front	Mar. L. A. Govorov	9	2	67	0	0	6	0	1
3rd Belorussian Front	Mar. A. M. Vasilevskiy	4	2	36	0	1	4	2	0
2nd Belorussian Front	Mar. K. K. Rokossovskiy	7	1	57	3	1	4	4	1
1st Belorussian Front	Mar. G. K. Zhukov	10	1	72	6	3	8	5	2
1st Ukrainian Front	Mar. I. S. Konev	12	1	82	3	1	8	6	4
4th Ukrainian Front	Gen. Army A. I. Yeremenko	4	1	33	0	0	2	1	0
2nd Ukrainian Front	Mar. R. Ya. Malinovskiy	7	1	45	9	1	4	2	3
3rd Ukrainian Front	Mar. F. I. Tolbukin	5	1	42	3	1	3	1	1
Total**		60	10	448	24	9	39	21	12

*Includes allied Polish, Romanian, and Bulgarian armies

**Includes independent armies

Soviet allied armies

The Red Army had four allied armies in the field in the final campaigns of 1945, totaling over a million additional troops. The Bulgarian and Romanian armies were both compelled to support the Red Army under the terms of their armistice agreements in 1944. They fought primarily in Hungary, Yugoslavia, and Czechoslovakia during the 1945 campaigns. The 1st Czechoslovak Army was a symbolic political effort. The most significant allied army was the Polish Peoples' Army (LWP: Ludowe Wojsko Polskie) that took part in the campaigns in Poland, Germany, and Czechoslovakia. The 1st Polish Army (1 AWP: 1 Armia Wojska Polskiego) saw its combat debut with the 1st Belorussian Front in central Poland in July 1944. With the entry of the Red Army into Poland in the summer of 1944, the LWP was substantially increased in size by conscription, forming the 2 AWP in July 1944. The Polish units were formed on the Red Army pattern with equipment establishments equivalent to Soviet Guards divisions. The LWP was most heavily committed at the time of the Oder–Vistula offensive in January 1945, and Polish divisions fought in both the Berlin and Prague campaigns. The LWP numbered 14 infantry divisions and one armored corps, totaling 400,000 troops by the end of the war.

RED ARMY ORDER OF BATTLE, MAY 1, 1945

Leningrad Front	**Marshal Leonid A. Govorov**
1st Shock Army	Gen. Lt. Vladimir Razubayev
4th Shock Army	Gen. Col. Petr Malyshev
6th Guards Army	Gen. Col. Ivan Chistyakov
10th Guards Army	Gen. Lt. Mikhail Kazakov
42nd Army	Gen. Lt. Vladimir Sviridov
51st Army	Gen. Lt. Vladimir Lvov
15th Air Army	Gen. Lt. Nikolai Naumenko
3rd Belorussian Front	**Marshal Aleksandr M. Vasilevskiy**
2nd Guards Army	Gen. Lt. Porfiriy Chanchibadze
11th Guards Army	Gen. Lt. Kuzma Galitskiy
48th Army	Gen. Lt. Nikolai Gusev
50th Army	Gen. Lt. Fedor Ozerov
1st Air Army	Gen. Col. Timofey Khryukin
3rd Air Army	Gen. Col. Stepan Krasovskiy
2nd Belorussian Front	**Marshal Konstantin K. Rokossovskiy**
2nd Shock Army	Gen. Lt. Ivan Fedyuninskiy
19th Army	Gen. Lt. Vladimir Romanovskiy
43rd Army	Gen. Lt. Afanasiy Beloborodov
49th Army	Gen. Col. Ivan Grishin
65th Army	Gen. Col. Pavel Batov
70th Army	Gen. Col. Vasiliy Popov
5th Guards Tank Army	Gen. Col. Vasiliy Volskiy
4th Air Army	Gen. Col. Konstantin Vershinin

1st Belorussian Front	**Marshal Georgi K. Zhukov**
3rd Shock Army	Gen. Lt. Kuzma Galitskiy
5th Shock Army	Gen. Col. Nikolai Berzarin
8th Guards Army	Gen. Col. Vasiliy Chuikov
3rd Army	Gen. Lt. Petr Pshennikov
33rd Army	Gen. Lt. Vasily Kryuchenkin
47th Army	Gen. Lt. Franz Perkhorovich
61st Army	Gen. Col. Pavel Belov
69th Army	Gen. Lt. Vladimir Kolpakchi
1st Guards Tank Army	Gen. Col. Mikhail Katukov
2nd Guards Tank Army	Gen. Col. Semen Bogdanov
1st Polish Army	Gen. Div. Stanisław Popławski
16th Air Army	Gen. Col. Sergey Rudenko
1st Ukrainian Front	**Marshal Ivan S. Konev**
3rd Guards Army	Gen. Col. Vasily Gordov
5th Guards Army	Gen. Col. Aleksey Zhadov
6th Army	Gen. Lt. Vladimir Gluzdovskiy
13th Army	Gen. Col. Nikolai Pukhov
21st Army	Gen. Col. Dmitriy Gusev
28th Army	Gen. Lt. Vasily Gerasimenko
31st Army	Gen. Lt. Petr Shafranov
52nd Army	Gen. Col. Konstantin Koroteyev
59th Army	Gen. Lt. Ivan Korovinkov
3rd Guards Tank Army	Gen. Col. Pavel Rybalko
4th Guards Tank Army	Gen. Lt. Dmitriy Lelyushenko
2nd Polish Army	Gen. Div. Karol Świerczewski

2nd Air Army	Gen. Col. Stepan Krasovskiy
4th Ukrainian Front	**Gen. Army Andrey I. Yeremenko**
1st Guards Army	Gen. Col. Andrei Grechko
18th Army	Gen. Lt. Anton Gastilovich
38th Army	Gen. Maj. Viktor Tsyganov
60th Army	Gen. Col. Pavel Kurochkin
6th Air Army	Gen. Lt. Fedor Polynin
2nd Ukrainian Front	**Marshal Rodion Ya. Malinovskiy**
7th Guards Army	Gen. Col. Mikhail Shumilov
40th Army	Gen. Lt. Filipp Zhmachenko
46th Army	Gen. Lt. Aleksandr Petrushevskiy
53rd Army	Gen. Col. Ivan Managarov
6th Guards Tank Army	Gen. Lt. Andrey Kravchenko
1st Guards Horse-Mechanized Group	Gen. Lt. Issa Pliyev
1st Romanian Army	Gen. Vasile Anastasiu
4th Romanian Army	Gen. Nicolae Dascalescu
3rd Ukrainian Front	**Marshal Fyodor I. Tolbukhin**
4th Guards Army	Gen. Lt. Nikanor Zakhvatayev
9th Guards Army	Gen. Col. Vasily Glagolev
26th Army	Gen. Lt. Nikolai Gagen
27th Army	Gen. Col. Sergey Trofimenko
57th Army	Gen. Lt. Dmitiy Ryadyshev
1st Bulgarian Army	Gen. Lt. Vladimir Stoichev
5th Air Army	Gen. Col. Sergey Goryunov
17th Air Army	Gen. Col. Vladimir Sudets

THE WESTERN ALLIES

Eisenhower's forces in the ETO (European Theater of Operations) consisted of three army groups with about 5 million troops.

Allied strength in the Northwest Europe Campaign, April 30, 1945

	Army	Air Force	Total
USA	2,618,020	447,480	3,065,500
Britain	835,200	460,000	1,295,200
France	413,140	24,000	437,140
Canada	183,420	34,000	217,420
Other Allies*	34,520	15,500	50,020
Other Commonwealth		12,500	12,500
Total	4,084,300	993,480	5,077,780

*Other Allies included Poland, Czechoslovakia, Netherlands, Belgium, and Norway

British and Commonwealth Forces
The British Army in Northwest Europe shrank from the time of the Normandy landings to the final campaigns of 1945 due to manpower shortages and overseas commitments in Italy, the Middle East and the Burma–India theater. In 1945, it totaled four armoured divisions, seven infantry divisions, and two airborne divisions. Montgomery's 21st Army Group was filled out by other formations with Canada providing two armoured divisions and three infantry

divisions; one Polish armoured division also served with the Canadians. There were also several small Allied formations attached, including the 1st Belgian Brigade, the Royal Netherlands Brigade, the Czechoslovak Armoured Brigade, and the 1st Polish Parachute Brigade.

British tank strength in NW Europe 1945

	January 27, 1945	May 5, 1945
Stuart	446	601
Sherman	1,247	1,373
Sherman 17-pdr	636	709
Cromwell	603	549
Challenger	25	30
Comet	35	237
Churchill	535	742
Total	3,527	4,241

21ST ARMY GROUP	**FIELD MARSHAL BERNARD L. MONTGOMERY**
I Airborne Corps	Lt. Gen. F. A. M. Browning
British Second Army	**Lt. Gen. Miles C. Dempsey**
30 Corps	Lt. Gen. B. G. Horrocks
12 Corps	Lt. Gen. N. M. Richie
8 Corps	Lt. Gen. E. H. Barker
Canadian First Army	**Lt. Gen. H. D. G. Crerar**
I British Corps	Lt. Gen J. T. Crocker
I Canadian Corps	Lt. Gen. C. Foulkes
II Canadian Corps	Lt. Gen. G. G. Simonds

US Army

The US Army in the European Theater of Operations (ETO) included 15 armored divisions, 42 infantry divisions and four airborne divisions by April–May 1945. Of the 68 infantry divisions raised in World War II, 42 were deployed to the ETO as well as all four of the airborne divisions. The US Army deployed 15 of its 16 armored divisions in the ETO; the only other one, the 1st Armored Division, was in Italy.

US Army ETO tank and AFV strength 1945

	January	February	March	April	May
M5A1	2,970	3,479	2,981	3,427	4,119
M24	20	128	364	736	1,163
M4 (75, 76mm)	4,561	5,297	6,249	5,727	6,336
M4 (105)	620	804	612	612	636
M26	0	20	20	60	108
Tank subtotal	8,171	9,728	10,226	10,562	12,362
M18	312	448	540	427	427
M10	768	686	684	427	427
M36	365	826	684	1,054	1,029
TD subtotal	1,445	1,960	1,908	1,908	1,883
Total	9,616	11,688	12,134	12,470	14,245

The French 1ere Armée Française was raised and equipped by the US Army and unit organization generally followed the US pattern. There were six infantry and three armored divisions committed to the campaign in Germany. The French divisions were raised in North Africa around colonial regiments. Additional divisions were formed in France after the summer of 1944 by absorbing resistance units into the army. However, these were mostly kept in France and delegated to lay siege to remaining German garrisons in the ports along the Atlantic coast including Lorient, St Nazaire, La Rochelle, and Royan.

12TH ARMY GROUP	**GEN. OMAR BRADLEY**
First US Army	**Gen. Courtney Hodges**
V Corps	Maj. Gen. Clarence Huebner
VII Corps	Maj. Gen. J. Lawton Collins
VIII Corps	Maj. Gen. Troy Middleton
XVIII Airborne Corps	Maj. Gen. Matthew Ridgway
Third US Army	**Gen. George Patton**
III Corps	Maj. Gen. James Van Fleet
XII Corps	Maj. Gen. Stafford Irwin
XX Corps	Maj. Gen. Walton Walker
Ninth US Army	**Lt. Gen. William Simpson**
XIII Corps	Maj. Gen. Alvan Gillem
XVI Corps	Maj. Gen. John Anderson
XIX Corps	Maj. Gen. Raymond McLain
Fifteenth US Army	**Lt. Gen. Leonard Gerow**
XXII Corps	Maj. Gen. Walton Walker
XXIII Corps	Maj. Gen. Hugh Gaffey
6TH ARMY GROUP	**GEN. JACOB DEVERS**
Seventh US Army	**Lt. Gen. Alexander Patch**
VI Corps	Maj. Gen. Edward Brooks
XV Corps	Maj. Gen. Wade Haislip
XXI Corps	Maj. Gen Frank Milburn
1ere Armée Française	**Gen. Jean de Lattre de Tassigny**
1e Corps	Lt. Gen. Emile Bethouart
2e Corps	Lt. Gen. Goislard de Montsabert

OPPOSING PLANS

GERMAN PLANS

German planning in the final months of the war was distorted by the conflicting perspectives of the senior Nazi Party leaders and army commanders. In the wake of the July 1944 coup attempt, Hitler's confidence in the military leadership was in continual decline, and he permitted growing interference in military matters by senior Nazi Party officials including Himmler, Goebbels, and Bormann. As the military situation became worse, Hitler increasingly abandoned any rational strategic planning and fell back on half-baked ideological panaceas such as the Volkssturm. Regional party officials were assigned as Reich Defense Commissars (RVK: Reichs Verteidigungs Kommissar) responsible for homeland defense, commanding the Volkssturm in the area behind the front lines. The *Alpenfestung* plan was another product of the Nazi Party officials, a German equivalent of the Soviet partisan war.

One of the bitterest arguments between Hitler and Guderian was over the dispersion of German forces around the periphery of Europe. This is the surrender of Panzer-Brigade "Norwegen" to British occupation forces in the Oslo area in the summer of 1945. (NARA)

Bavaria had been the birthplace of the Nazi Party and so it emerged as the center of a Wagnerian fantasy of a last-ditch stand in the Alpine fastness by die-hard Nazi fanatics.

Hitler saw the war as a Manichean struggle of the German people against the racially inferior Slavs. He convinced himself that victory depended on the fanatical will to resist. As a result, he would not countenance any withdrawal, no matter how prudent. On January 19, 1945, he instructed army commanders that any retreat of large units required his personal approval. During the fighting in early 1945, Hitler repeatedly designated many cities and towns as "*Festung*" to be defended to the last man. This robbed the German Army of its tactical flexibility.

The OKW chief of staff, Heinz Guderian, was one of the last German commanders willing to argue with Hitler over operational plans. Guderian's main strategic objection to Hitler's plans was the excessive dispersion of Germany's limited resources, and the failure to adequately reinforce the Berlin axis, the main focal point of the Soviet advance. He had strongly opposed the Ardennes offensive as a waste of Germany's last mobile reserves, and favored their deployment on the Warsaw–Berlin axis. When Hitler finally approved the transfer of the 6. Panzer-Armee to the east, he again urged its deployment along the Berlin axis. Instead, Hitler deployed it on the Budapest–Vienna axis to the south, throwing it away on yet another pointless counteroffensive.

Guderian also favored a strategic retrenchment of German forces to bolster the Eastern Front. He strongly opposed the retention of more than 20 divisions in the Kurland pocket on Latvia's Baltic coast. Hitler argued that the Kurland pocket tied down Soviet forces; Guderian argued that the Red Army had ample divisions that could be wasted on containing the Kurland pocket while Germany could not afford such a drain. Aside from the 20 divisions tied down in the Kurland pocket, the Wehrmacht had about 40 divisions in peripheral theaters including Norway, Italy, and the Balkans; Hitler refused to pull any of these forces back for a final defense of the Reich. One of Guderian's few small victories in his struggles with Hitler was his effort to replace Himmler as commander of the vital Heeregruppe Weichsel on the approaches to Berlin. Hitler forced Guderian to retire on March 28, 1945.

Hitler's outlook had grown increasingly nihilistic in 1945 as he realized that Germany was on the brink of defeat. He blamed Germany's misfortune on the betrayal of the army leadership and the German people. His bitterness was manifest in his decisions to ensure massive destruction within Germany rather than contemplate surrender. The most notorious of these was the so-called Nero Directive, more formally entitled the "Directive on the Demolitions on Reich Territory" (*Befehl betreffend Zerstörungsmaßnahmen im Reichsgebiet*) issued on March 19, 1945. He ordered that "All military transport and communication facilities, factories and supply depots, as well as anything else of value within Reich territory, which could in any way be used by the enemy immediately or within the foreseeable future for the prosecution of the war, will be destroyed." He entrusted the program to Albert Speer, the Minister of War Production, who was appalled at the potential consequences for Germany after the war. Speer took steps to minimize this senseless destruction, though there was substantial demolition of bridges and other infrastructure in the final months of the war during the course of military operations.

ALLIED PLANS

The Yalta conference in February 1945 established the basic strategic considerations for military operations in the final months of the war. The conference reaffirmed the policy of unconditional surrender on all fronts and the rejection of any German attempt to halt operations in one theater while permitting continuing military operations elsewhere. The Soviet Union was concerned that Germany would attempt to negotiate a cease-fire in the west while continuing to resist the advance of the Red Army.

Western Allied plans

The protracted debate in Anglo-American military planning had been centered around Montgomery's scheme to concentrate Allied resources with his army group in the north as the principal focal point of the advance. Eisenhower opposed this approach, fearing that a single thrust offered the Germans an opportunity to concentrate their reduced resources in a single sector. Eisenhower preferred a broad-front approach by all three army groups advancing in parallel to place maximum stress on the depleted Wehrmacht.

With the elimination of the Ruhr pocket underway, the next issue to be resolved was the focus of the final endgame. Montgomery continued to urge a concentration of Allied resources in the north with the ultimate aim of

Eisenhower was concerned that the Germans planned to prolong the war by staging a last-ditch defense in a "National Redoubt" in the Alps. This Seventh US Army G-2 assessment from March 25, 1945 forecast a gradual German retreat southward through a succession of defense positions as depicted on this map.

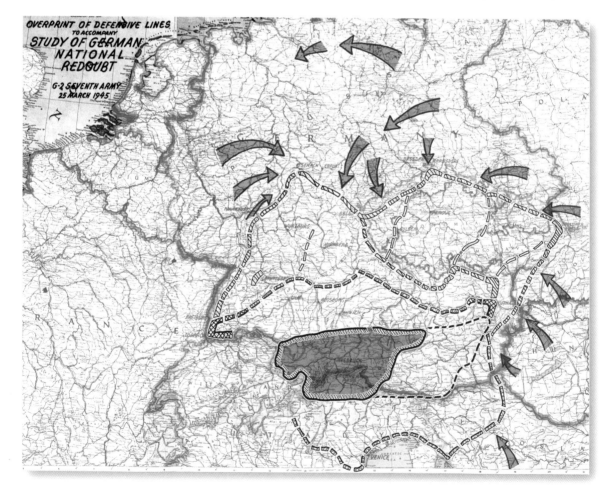

making a dash for Berlin. Eisenhower had originally supported Berlin as the ultimate Allied objective, but developments in 1945 had moved him away from this goal. The Yalta conference placed Berlin in the Soviet occupation zone, and any advance on the city raised the specter of a fratricidal encounter between Anglo-American and Soviet forces in the vicinity of Berlin. By late March 1945, the Red Army was significantly closer to Berlin than the nearest US and British forces. Eisenhower was also skeptical of Montgomery's depiction of a lightning thrust towards Berlin in view of the British general's preference for carefully staged offensive operations, the lugubrious pace of Operation *Varsity–Plunder* in March 1945 being the latest example.

Montgomery's assertion of the leadership role in a Berlin operation exacerbated long-standing tensions with US commanders. Bradley was irritated by Montgomery's pattern of having American field armies detached from his 12th Army Group and subordinated to Montgomery's command. Simpson's Ninth US Army had only returned to Bradley's command on March 28 at the conclusion of the Rhine crossing operations and Bradley had directed it to the reduction of the Ruhr pocket. A simple glance at the map suggested that the Allied field armies most likely to be employed towards Berlin would be the Ninth US Army in the center and the First US Army in the south.

Other factors undermined Eisenhower's interest in a thrust to Berlin. By the beginning of April 1945, it was likely that the war in Europe would be over in a month or two. A significant portion of the US units in the ETO was earmarked for transfer to the Pacific for an eventual amphibious invasion of Japan. Recent operations in the Pacific such as the Philippines, Iwo Jima, and Okinawa had been extremely costly, and there was every reason to suspect that Operation *Downfall*, the anticipated amphibious landings in Japan, would involve massive army casualties. Eisenhower asked Bradley about the cost of a thrust from the Elbe to Berlin and he estimated 100,000 casualties, "a pretty stiff price for a prestige objective."

In addition, there were anxieties over German plans for the final endgame. There had been hints from the intelligence services that the Nazi Party planned to conduct a prolonged campaign of partisan warfare even after the Wehrmacht had been vanquished. There had been hints that die-hards of the Nazi Party planned to create a "National Redoubt" in southern Germany, the American name for the *Alpenfestung* scheme.

Eisenhower decided that the principal objective should be a rapid destruction of the German Army to end the war as quickly as possible; Berlin was a costly distraction from this goal. Each of the three army groups under his command would have distinct objectives. Montgomery's 21st Army Group would conclude the liberation of the Netherlands, and make a rapid thrust toward the Baltic with an aim of liberating Denmark before the arrival of the Red Army. Bradley's 12th Army Group would advance to the Elbe and await the arrival of the Red Army. Devers' 6th Army Group, reinforced with Patton's Third US Army, would head to the southeast to prevent the establishment of a National Redoubt, while at the same time advancing into Austria as circumstances permitted.

On March 28, 1945, Eisenhower asked the Allied military mission in Moscow to convey an outline of this plan to Stalin. This triggered a bitter political exchange between British and American military and political leaders, with the British chief-of-staff, Field Marshal Alan Brooke, still advocating a thrust to Berlin. Eisenhower formally presented his plans to the Combined Chiefs of Staff on April 7 noting that "I regard it as unsound at this stage of the proceedings to make Berlin a major objective, particularly in view of the fact that it is only 35 miles from the Russian lines. I am the first to admit that a war is waged in pursuance of political aims, and if the Combined Chiefs of Staff should decide that the Allied effort to take Berlin outweighs purely military considerations in this theater, I would cheerfully readjust my plans and my thinking so as to carry out such an operation." The CCS deferred to Eisenhower's judgment, settling the debate.

Soviet plans

Red Army operations in March and early April succeeded in clearing the most serious threats along the northern flanks in Pomerania and Prussia, though isolated ports and fortress cities continued to resist. In the south, the Red Army reached Vienna by the end of March, entering the city on April 13–15. In the center, the fortress city of Küstrin was encircled on March 22–23, creating a solid bridgehead over the Oder for the future drive of the 1st Belorussian Front on Berlin.

Eisenhower's letter on March 28, 1945 triggered the Soviet decision to accelerate the Berlin operation. Although Eisenhower had explicitly ruled out an advance on Berlin by Anglo-American forces, Stalin regarded this as a ruse to mask the actual intentions of the "little allies." Stalin responded to Eisenhower by affirming the decision to meet along the Elbe, but he disingenuously suggested that the Soviet focus had shifted from Berlin to Leipzig.

Zhukov and Konev were recalled to Moscow to begin discussions on the conduct of the operation, and met with Stalin and the Stavka on April 1; Rokossovskiy arrived on April 2. The plan was to stage a massive breakthrough operation by Zhukov's 1st Belorussian Front in the center and Konev's 1st Ukrainian Front in the south. Berlin would be encircled and the city's defenses systematically reduced. Rokossovskiy's 2nd Belorussian Front would clear northeastern Germany. Preparations for the assault were most difficult in the northern sector since Rokossovskiy's forces had been heavily engaged in the reduction of Danzig, about 500km from the Oder start line and as a result, they started later. The plan expected the operation would take 12–15 days to complete.

THE CAMPAIGN

THE RUHR POCKET

The Anglo-American forces launched a series of coordinated offensives in the third week of March 1945 to cross the Rhine. Montgomery's Operation *Plunder*, beginning on March 24, was the most elaborate and lavish Allied operation since the D-Day landings, involving the entire British 21st Army Group with a combined force of over a million troops and over 30 divisions, complete with a subordinate airborne landing, Operation *Varsity*. Simpson's Ninth US Army was detached from Bradley's 12th Army Group to Montgomery's command to conduct Operation *Flashpoint* to cover the southern flank of the British river crossing. Bradley's 12th Army Group launched Operation *Voyage*, the breakout from the Remagen bridgehead area. Although scheduled to begin a day later than Operation *Plunder*, Bradley had authorized Patton to bounce the Rhine when the opportunity presented itself on March 22–23 near Oppenheim.

Bradley's attack south of the Ruhr proceeded faster than expected, aided by the mistaken focus of German defenses around the Remagen bridgehead. Generalfeldmarschall Walter Model, the commander of Heeresgruppe B, expected that the focal point of the Remagen breakout would be at the northern shoulder to permit the First US Army to roll up the Rhine and meet up with the Ninth US Army before pressing an attack against the Ruhr industrial zone. In fact, the focus of the First US Army attack was in the south, with the aim of seizing and exploiting the autobahn in that area.

Model's dilemma was not only a mistaken appreciation of the American intent, but also the profound weakness of his forces. Heeresgruppe B had suffered crippling casualties during the retreat over the Rhine in March 1945, and had received few replacements. The front along the Rhine was held by token forces of 5. Panzer-Armee with about six understrength divisions with a density of only about 15 soldiers per kilometer. The perimeter around the Remagen bridgehead was defended by 15. Armee with 14 divisions, labeled as *Kampfgruppen* in army records due to their perilous state. They had a density of about 80 troops per kilometer. The entire army group had only two divisions in reserve. On the positive side, there was ample artillery, reinforced by large numbers of heavy Flak batteries covering the numerous industrial cities in the region. A day before the attack, Berlin ordered Model to relinquish 11. Panzer-Division to Heeresgruppe G to the south to deal with Patton's unanticipated leapfrog of the Rhine. As a result, Model's tank strength was a paltry 65 Panzers, about 50 along the front and 15 in reserve.

In contrast, the opposing US units were amply equipped. For example, Simpson's Ninth US Army had 1,170 M4 medium tanks and 620 light tanks; Hodges' First US Army had 1,050 M4 medium tanks and 625 light tanks.

The Ninth US Army launched its attack in conjunction with Montgomery's Operation *Plunder* in the pre-dawn hours of March 24 with an hour-long artillery preparation against the defenses of the 180. Infanterie-Division between Wesel and Dinslaken. The German defenders were shell-shocked by the intensity of the bombardment. Infantry crossings of the Rhine were conducted using assault boats supported by LVT amphibious tractors and amphibious DD tanks. Heavy equipment was carried using LCVP and LCM landing craft that had been laboriously trucked to the Rhine from the North Sea. By early morning, two infantry divisions were across the river to a depth of 5–7km. Casualties had been light due to the devastating artillery preparation. The 180. Infanterie-Division had been shattered, with more than 2,000 prisoners taken on the first day of the offensive.

Hodges' First US Army initiated Operation *Voyage* in the pre-dawn hours of March 25. The attack was launched out of the Remagen bridgehead with three corps, including five infantry and two armored divisions. Within a few hours after the start of the attack, Model's headquarters had lost contact with LXXIV. Armee-Korps and LXVII. Armee-Korps, which had both been largely overwhelmed. The focus of the American attack had fallen on LXVII. Korps, which was so thoroughly overrun that Gen. Hitzfeld ordered a general retreat. The corps disintegrated and did not manage to contact Heeregruppe B for nearly a week, by which time its paltry remnants were scattered around Fulda. Generaloberst Püchler's LXXIV. Korps had attempted to pull back to the second line of defenses but was completely disrupted; the remnants of the 9. Panzer-Division were overwhelmed and 340. Volksgrenadier-Division was destroyed. The First US Army had secured a sizeable breakthrough in a single day, and Heeresgruppe B was unaware of the depth of the American penetration.

To make matters even worse, the 4th Armored Division from Patton's Third US Army had broken out of the Oppenheim bridgehead to the south, cleared the Main River, and was heading north to link up with the First US Army. Generaloberst Höhne's LXXXIX. Armee-Korps became trapped between the First and Third US armies, and its collapse in the face of the sequential attacks left a gaping hole between Heeresgruppen B and G.

The Allied offensives on March 24–25 threatened to isolate Heeresgruppe B from Heeresgruppe H to the north and Heeresgruppe G to the south. Model was fully aware that Hitler would not countenance any retreat so he carefully phrased a request to Kesselring's OB West headquarters asking for a "new mission." While awaiting a

A patrol from the 137th Infantry, 35th Infantry Division, clears a block in the city of Hern on April 9, 1945 during the reduction of the Ruhr pocket. (NARA)

response, he reconfigured the Ruhr defenses. The sector along the Rhine was not threatened by the American forces and could be held by a light screening force. The sector in the north, especially the northwest, was a dense agglomeration of industrial cities such as Dusseldorf and Essen that could be held with modest infantry forces backed by extensive Flak positions. The sector to the south and east was rural and forested, and would be the most vulnerable to American attack. This sector would be vital for any attempt to connect with German forces outside the Ruhr, or for any breakout attempt. Not surprisingly, Model decided to focus his defensive efforts with Gen. Zangen's 15. Armee along the Sieg and Lahn rivers facing south and east. However, communications with 15. Armee headquarters proved nearly impossible for several days. About the only coherent force still left in this sector was Gen. Bayerlein's battered LIII. Korps.

On March 26, Model visited Bayerlein and instructed him to prepare a counterattack against the northern flank of the First US Army advance. Bayerlein protested that he had no mobile forces to conduct such a mission after 11. Panzer-Division had been sent south; Model responded with an abusive tirade. The confrontation convinced Bayerlein that it was pointless to try to discuss issues with Model; in the future he would simply agree with Model's directives whether he intended to carry them out or not. Model had no clear appreciation of the situation south of the Sieg River. Still unwilling to accept the unfolding disaster, Model ordered Bayerlein to withdraw his forces towards Siegen, take command of the remaining armored strength of the army group, and prepare a southward counterattack across the three US corps to Limburg. Bayerlein called the order "impossible, entirely hopeless, and insane." Model eventually realized the futility of any counterattack southward, and instead ordered Bayerlein to join the defense line on the Sieg River.

OB West refused Model's request for "a new mission" after they learned that Hitler had declared that the Festung Ruhr (Fortress Ruhr) was to be defended to the last bullet with no option of retreat. Hitler ordered that a new 12. Armee would be formed to link up with Heeresgruppe B. Model still was uncertain whether the First US Army would join up with Patton's Third US Army and proceed to the southeast and away from the Ruhr, or whether it would eventually swing northeast and join up instead with the Ninth US Army, trapping Heeresgruppe B. In fact, Bradley intended to do both. On March 28, Bradley initiated a shallow envelopment of the Ruhr and ordered the First US Army to turn Collins' VII Corps north towards Paderborn to meet up with the Ninth US Army.

On March 29, Model outlined several options to OB West. As a short-term expedient, he recommended a counterattack from the eastern sector around Winterberg with an aim of blunting the drive by Collins' VII Corps towards Paderborn and retaining contact with the Wehrkreis IX in Kassel and the 11. Armee in the Harz Mountain area. On the night of March 29–30, Kesselring's OB West headquarters responded. The mission remained the defense of the Ruhr and the Rhine and, by Hitler's direct order, withdrawal of Heeresgruppe B was out of the question. The Winterberg counterattack was approved, but in reality there were not enough forces to conduct anything more than a modest spoiling attack.

By Good Friday, March 30, 1945, the German counterattack was ready to be launched. Bayerlein's LIII. Korps was relieved of its defensive responsibilities and the new SS-Panzer-Ersatz brigade "Westfalen" was created, using troops from the Waffen-SS Panzer and Panzer reconnaissance schools at Sennelager, north of Paderborn. The brigade consisted of two improvised infantry regiments and a single tank company using 15 old training tanks. Its main armored element was s.Pz.Abt. 507, an experienced Tiger battalion that was at Sennelager to replenish after its heavy losses on the Russian Front. It had only 21 Kingtigers and three Jagdpanthers on hand. This hastily improvised brigade deployed south of Paderborn in the early morning hours of Good Friday with the intention of blocking the American armored spearheads heading towards the city.

Bayerlein's LIII. Korps attack began from the Winterberg area towards the Edertalsperre on the evening of 30 March consisting of two *Kampfgruppen* of infantry and pioneers supported by 12 Panzers, a few assault guns, but no artillery. Instead of cutting behind the rear of the 3rd Armored Division as expected, the German units ran into an improvised motorized infantry task force of the 104th Division. Model's desperate counterattack fizzled out as a mere nuisance raid. Fighting broke out between SS-Panzer-Brigade "Westfalen" and the spearheads of 3rd Armored Division on the southern approaches to Paderborn on March 31. This was the first serious resistance encountered in a week of fighting, and the divisional commander, Maj. Gen. Maurice Rose, was killed later that day in a chance encounter with a Kingtiger tank.

Impatient with the delays around Paderborn, Lt. Gen. J. Lawton Collins skirted official channels and directly contacted Lt. Gen. William Simpson of the Ninth US Army with the proposal that they each dispatch an armored task force towards Lippstadt to link up and complete the encirclement. Combat Command B of the 2nd Armored Division met Task Force Kane from the 3rd Armored Division around 1530hrs on Easter Sunday, April 1, 1945, encircling the Ruhr pocket.

A typical scene from the spring 1945 fighting during the reduction of the Ruhr. Even though numerous white blankets fly from the windows of, the GI in the foreground had been hit by rifle fire from within the town. In response, other GIs from the 44th Armored Infantry Battalion advance cautiously behind a M4A3E8 medium tank of Task Force 44, 6th Armored Division, in Oberdorla, Germany on April 4, 1945, hunting out the last defenders. (NARA)

REDUCING FESTUNG RUHR

Once Operation *Voyage* had encircled the Ruhr, the new Fifteenth US Army was assigned to patrol the Rhine sector until it was strong enough to free the other two field armies to continue to advance eastward. Bradley assumed that a significant number of German troops were encircled, but the expectation was that most of Heeresgruppe B would have escaped and that only about 70,000 troops would be left in the pocket. Bradley had not anticipated Hitler's stand-fast orders, and in fact the pocket contained about 370,000 German troops, although the actual combat value of the forces within the Ruhr was

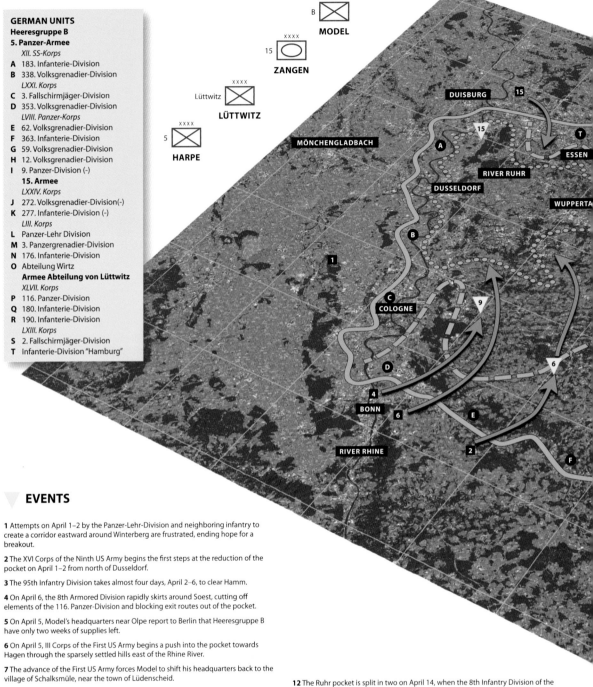

GERMAN UNITS
Heeresgruppe B
5. Panzer-Armee
XII. SS-Korps
A 183. Infanterie-Division
B 338. Volksgrenadier-Division
LXXI. Korps
C 3. Fallschirmjäger-Division
D 353. Volksgrenadier-Division
LVIII. Panzer-Korps
E 62. Volksgrenadier-Division
F 363. Infanterie-Division
G 59. Volksgrenadier-Division
H 12. Volksgrenadier-Division
I 9. Panzer-Division (-)
15. Armee
LXXIV. Korps
J 272. Volksgrenadier-Division(-)
K 277. Infanterie-Division (-)
LIII. Korps
L Panzer-Lehr Division
M 3. Panzergrenadier-Division
N 176. Infanterie-Division
O Abteilung Wirtz
Armee Abteilung von Lüttwitz
XLVII. Korps
P 116. Panzer-Division
Q 180. Infanterie-Division
R 190. Infanterie-Division
LXIII. Korps
S 2. Fallschirmjäger-Division
T Infanterie-Division "Hamburg"

▼ EVENTS

1 Attempts on April 1–2 by the Panzer-Lehr-Division and neighboring infantry to create a corridor eastward around Winterberg are frustrated, ending hope for a breakout.

2 The XVI Corps of the Ninth US Army begins the first steps at the reduction of the pocket on April 1–2 from north of Dusseldorf.

3 The 95th Infantry Division takes almost four days, April 2–6, to clear Hamm.

4 On April 6, the 8th Armored Division rapidly skirts around Soest, cutting off elements of the 116. Panzer-Division and blocking exit routes out of the pocket.

5 On April 5, Model's headquarters near Olpe report to Berlin that Heeresgruppe B have only two weeks of supplies left.

6 On April 5, III Corps of the First US Army begins a push into the pocket towards Hagen through the sparsely settled hills east of the Rhine River.

7 The advance of the First US Army forces Model to shift his headquarters back to the village of Schalksmüle, near the town of Lüdenscheid.

8 The return of clear weather frees up the IX and XXIX Tactical Air Commands to provide air support, but there are strict orders to limit strikes on railroad rolling stock north of the Ruhr River.

9 On April 12, the newly arrived 13th Armored Division sees its combat debut.

10 The headquarters of the 15. Armee and LXXXI. Korps surrenders to the 7th Armored Division on April 13.

11 On April 14, the 7th Armored Division captures Stalag VI-A Hemer/Iserlohn, freeing about 23,300 prisoners of war.

12 The Ruhr pocket is split in two on April 14, when the 8th Infantry Division of the First US Army and the 75th Division of the Ninth US Army reach the Ruhr River at Hattingen.

13 Panzer-Lehr-Division surrenders to the 99th Division on April 15, largely ending the fighting in the area of the eastern pocket.

14 The western portion of the pocket containing the remnants of 5. Panzer-Armee and the headquarters of Heeresgruppe B begins a precipitous collapse on April 18.

15 On April 21 GFM Model goes alone into the woods between Duisburg and the village of Lintorf, and shoots himself.

THE REDUCTION OF THE RUHR POCKET
April 1–18, 1945

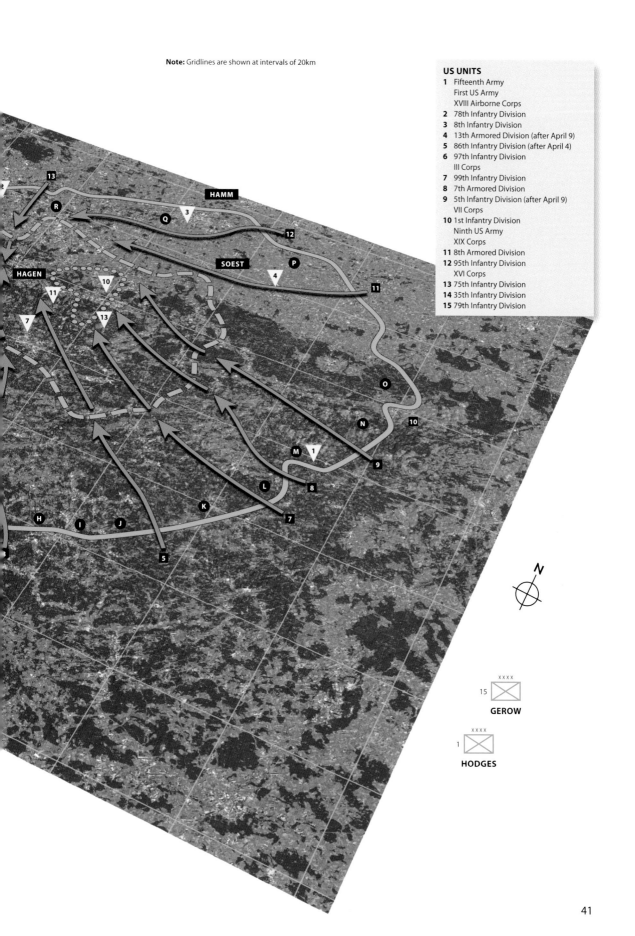

US UNITS
1 Fifteenth Army
  First US Army
  XVIII Airborne Corps
2 78th Infantry Division
3 8th Infantry Division
4 13th Armored Division (after April 9)
5 86th Infantry Division (after April 4)
6 97th Infantry Division
  III Corps
7 99th Infantry Division
8 7th Armored Division
9 5th Infantry Division (after April 9)
  VII Corps
10 1st Infantry Division
  Ninth US Army
  XIX Corps
11 8th Armored Division
12 95th Infantry Division
  XVI Corps
13 75th Infantry Division
14 35th Infantry Division
15 79th Infantry Division

HAMM

SOEST

HAGEN

GEROW

HODGES

41

much less than this figure would suggest. The pocket contained large numbers of rear service troops and Luftwaffe Flak crews. Only 20 percent of the troops had infantry weapons, another 20 percent had only pistols. Requests for airlift of supplies was denied, knowing full well that any such attempt would evaporate in the face of overwhelming Allied airpower. Although Hitler was under the delusion that Festung Ruhr could hold out for months, Model's headquarters estimated that food and supplies would last for only about three weeks since there was a large civilian population to consider.

Hitler had promised to relieve the pocket using the battered 11. Armee and the embryonic 12. Armee. General Walter Lucht's 11. Armee was a field army in name only. It had the headquarter staffs of two corps but its strength was only the decimated 166. Infanterie-Division recently arrived from occupation duty in Denmark, the remnants of SS-Panzer-Brigade "Westfalen," an assault gun battalion, and a ragtag assortment of replacement battalions.

By April 2, Model had lost contact with Heeresgruppe H to the north since it had been pushed back by the British offensives. The city of Kassel was enveloped by the Third US Army and fell on April 4, effectively ending any hope of relief from the east. On April 5, Model reported to Berlin that Heeresgruppe B had two weeks of supplies left and the situation was critical in regards to fuel and ammunition. Another request to authorize withdrawal was rejected.

The Ruhr defenses centered around towns and villages, with an especially vigorous defense at the eastern end of the pocket. After the first few days, German resistance began to sharply decrease and the number of prisoners-of-war increased. The average US advance into the pocket was 6–10km per day. After a week of fighting, the Ruhr defenses began to disintegrate. The Ninth US Army had a tough time penetrating into the industrial wasteland on the north side of the pocket, not only because of its dense urban infrastructure, but due to the enormous damage caused by over a year of intense heavy bombing raids by the RAF. Progress was far better in the First US Army sector to the south. On April 9, over 9,700 prisoners were taken by the First US Army; XVI Corps took another 10,000. On April 14, the 8th Infantry Division of the First US Army reached the Ruhr River at Hattingen;

One of the most shocking discoveries for the Allies during the April 1945 operations in western Germany was the numerous concentration camps. This is one of the mass graves at the Bergen-Belsen concentration camp. The British 11th Armoured Division liberated the camp on April 15, 1945. (NARA)

across the river was the 75th Division of the Ninth US Army. The junction of these forces broke the Ruhr pocket in half.

The dissection of the Ruhr pocket convinced Model that any further organized resistance was futile. Zangen and the remaining staff of the 15. Armee surrendered on April 13, Panzer Lehr Division on April 15. Model refused to surrender Heeresgruppe B but euphemistically referred to its "dissolution." Underage and overage troops were issued formal discharge papers on April 15; on April 17 the remaining soldiers were allowed to surrender on their own volition or try to fight their way out in groups. The pocket largely collapsed by April 18. In total, some 317,000 German troops surrendered in the Ruhr, a greater total than even Stalingrad or Tunisia. Model told his staff that "a field marshal does not surrender," and he reflected that "I sincerely believe that I have served a criminal. I led my soldiers in good conscience but for a criminal government." On April 21 he went alone into the woods and shot himself. The destruction of Heeresgruppe B, the main German force in the west, left an enormous gap in German defenses.

RACE TO THE ELBE

The destruction of Heeresgruppe B in the Ruhr pocket marked the end of large-scale operations by the Wehrmacht in the west. Kesselring, the OB West commander, called the final weeks of fighting in the west a "makeshift campaign" – a disjointed effort to conduct local defensive actions by what few divisions had sufficient morale to continue the fight under such hopeless circumstances. The outcome by now was obvious.

By the second week of April, Bradley's 12th Army Group became the largest field command in US Army history with four field armies, 12 corps and 48 divisions totaling 1.3 million troops. The newly arrived Fifteenth US Army was left behind in the Ruhr pocket while the other three armies raced east. Simpson's Ninth US Army remained on the northern flank, also covering the right flank of the British advance while advancing north of the forested Harz Mountain region. Hodges' First US Army was in the center, skirting along the southern side of the Harz Mountains and aimed at Leipzig. Patton's Third US Army aimed for the Elbe around Chemnitz.

German defenses at this stage of the war were entirely unpredictable. The civilians in most towns and villages were anxious for the war to end, and white flags popped up prior to the arrival of US forces. But this could be dangerous if die-hard German troops were nearby, and numerous German soldiers and civilians were executed for defeatism even in the last weeks of the war. Many German cities had heavy Flak batteries deployed around them, and these often formed the basis of a vigorous if short-lived defense effort.

One of the last major river lines in central Germany, the Weser, had all of its bridges blown. The 2nd Armored Division under the Ninth US Army was the first over the river on April 5, and then became the first to reach the Elbe on April 11. Other divisions soon followed. The 83rd Division, nicknamed the 83rd Armored Division because of its use of a fleet of captured German vehicles, was the next to the river near Barby. The First US Army reached the Weser on April 7 while facing the remnants of the 11. Armee. On April 8, Kesselring informed 11. Armee that they were to withdraw into Festung Harz and create an impregnable defense in the forested mountain region in anticipation of the

Advance to the Elbe, April 1945

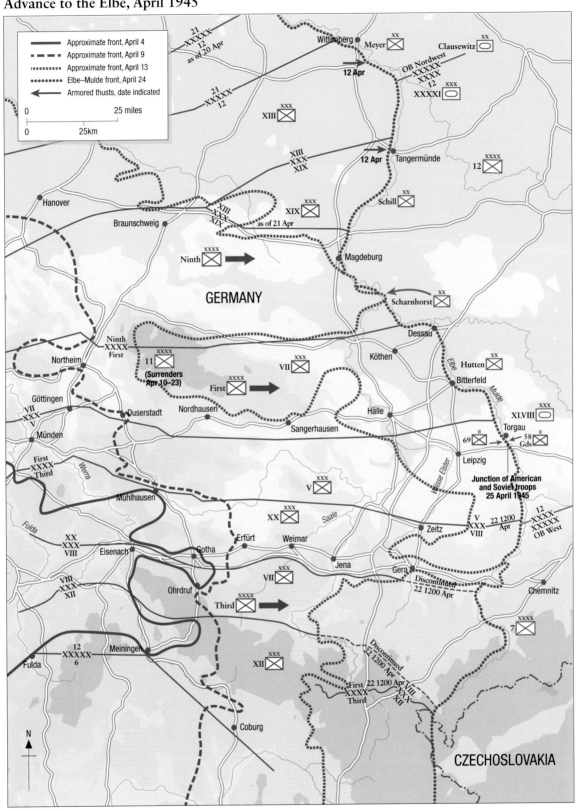

arrival of 12. Armee. The 11. Armee had barely arrived over the Leine River when armored spearheads of the First US Army jumped the river.

The rapid advance into central Germany began to uncover the dark secret of the concentration camps. These were not death camps like those in Poland that had been purpose-built to destroy Europe's Jews. Nevertheless, they were the scene of shocking levels of brutality and death. One of the worst, at Nordhausen, was reached on April 11.

The last effort to establish a new defense west of Berlin was the creation of 12. Armee under Gen. der Panzertruppe Walter Wenck. Hitler had created this formation from Germany's last scraps of troops and equipment. On paper, the field army consisted of three corps headquarters, a Panzer division, a Panzergrenadier division, and five or more infantry divisions. Since none of these divisions had been formed at the time of the army's activation, Wenck never possessed a real field army, but simply a scattering of slap-dash units. The first units were formed in the vicinity of the Harz Mountains. Panzer-Division "von Clausewitz" was created from the Panzer training school at Putlos and the embryonic 233. Ersatz-Panzer-Division from Denmark. It had at least 47 tanks and over a dozen assault guns; many of the tanks were obsolete or experimental types used at Putlos for training. The infantry units, quickly dubbed the "childrens' divisions," were formed using teenage conscripts of the RAD (Reichsarbeitdienst: National Work Service) with small cadres of experienced officers and NCOs, and remnants of shattered infantry units.

As the newly formed divisions arrived, the 12. Armee gradually deployed them along the Elbe front. Kesselring's OB West headquarters had assessed the Ninth US Army as the main threat and the focal point of the Allied advance. The expectation was that the Ninth US Army would send an armored spearhead to the western suburbs of Berlin while the rest of the American forces waited along the Elbe. As a result, the first clashes between the 12. Armee and Ninth US Army took place around the Elbe bridgeheads south of Magdeburg. The main German attack was conducted against the small Elbe bridgehead held by two infantry battalions of the 2nd Armored

The crew of a Cromwell tank of the British 7th Armoured Division in Hamburg after the city's surrender on May 3, 1945. The crewman sitting on the tank with a German MP.38 machine pistol is actually a Russian soldier who the crew had liberated days before at the Osnabrück camp and who served with the tank through the war's end. (NARA)

Division. The German attack was supported by heavy artillery fire from neighboring Flak batteries that smashed all attempts to put bridges across. After suffering nearly 300 casualties, the 2nd Armored Division decided that the bridgehead was not worth the cost and withdrew to the western bank on April 14. Repeated attacks against the larger bridgehead of the 83rd Division by the newly formed Division "Scharnhorst" were less successful.

The weakness of the German defenses along the Elbe convinced the Ninth US Army that Berlin was within easy reach. The staff had come up with a plan "to enlarge the bridgeheads over the Elbe to include Potsdam." Since Potsdam was within Berlin's suburbs, this required permission from higher commands. Simpson visited Bradley's headquarters on April 15, who in turn radioed Eisenhower. His response was unequivocal – no advance on Berlin. The 12. Armee still held the city of Magdeburg, and after preliminary air bombardment on April 17, the city fell to the 30th Division on April 18.

Kesselring ordered 12. Armee to continue their mission of reaching the Harz Mountains, and the assignment was given to Arndt's XXXIX. Panzer-Korps, consisting mainly of Panzer-Division "von Clausewitz" supported by some elements of the partially formed Panzergrenadier-Division "Schlageter z.b.V.1." In view of the fighting in Magdeburg and the bridgeheads south of the city, the attempt was made further north near the junction between the British 2nd Army and the Ninth US Army's XIII Corps. Panzer-Division "von Clausewitz" was deployed in three *Kampfgruppen*, the northernmost of which bumped into the British 15th Division near Ülzen on April 14. In a sharp encounter, Clausewitz lost ten assault guns and ten armored half-tracks. The other *Kampfgruppen* attempted to infiltrate through XIII Corps lines further south, and on April 16, one force with about 30 tanks and 1,000 troops cut one of the main XIII Corps supply roads near the Klötzer forest. The 5th Armored Division was sent to finish off the division and it was largely destroyed by April 21.

The 11. Armee held a dwindling refuge in the Harz pocket. Although Lucht's command included about 70,000 troops, they had little artillery and few tanks. US infantry operations against the pocket began on April 11, encountering numerous roadblocks on the mountain roads. On April 18, the 1st Division captured the highest point in the mountains at Brocken and, by April 20, some 18,000 troops had surrendered. Lucht and his headquarters were captured on April 23, bringing Festung Harz to an end.

A M4 medium tank of the US 7th Armored Division dips its tracks in the Baltic near Wismar in early May 1945. The XVIII Airborne Corps formed the extreme eastern wing of the advance of Montgomery's 21st Army Group to reach the Danish frontier ahead of the Red Army. (NARA)

EASTERN FRONT: PREPARING FOR BERLIN

The Red Army had finally cleared Festung Küstrin on March 28, providing a bridgehead over the Oder immediately facing Berlin. In the other sectors, the Red Army would have to create tactical bridging over the Oder and Neisse rivers. In the center, Zhukov's 1st Belorussian Front had seven Soviet, one Polish, and two tank armies with 986,500 troops. This force was located in the Küstrin bridgehead aimed directly at Berlin. To its immediate south, Konev's 1st Ukrainian Front had five Soviet, one Polish, and two tank armies with a further 628,900 troops. This force deployed on either side of Festung Cottbus with an intention of securing the southern approaches to Berlin and reaching the Elbe. There was a gap between the two fronts since the many small lakes southeast of Berlin precluded a mechanized advance; this gap was covered by two static defense sectors (UR: *Ukreplenniy rayon*). Rokossovskiy's 2nd Belorussian Front was to the north with five Soviet armies and about 441,600 troops. Due to the delay in moving its forces from the Baltic coast, it was scheduled to start its attack a few days after the other with an intention of overrunning German positions in the port of Stettin and then proceeding to the Elbe to the north of Berlin. Soviet and allied Polish forces started the Berlin operation with about 1.9 million combat troops, 21 corps, 171 divisions, plus 6,250 tanks and assault guns.

The principal German forces on the Berlin axis were Heeresgruppe Weichsel and Heeresgruppe Mitte. These two army groups plus the Berlin garrison numbered 770,000 German troops along with 425 tanks and 1,070 assault guns and tank destroyers for a total of 1,495 AFVs. The forces facing Zhukov's 1st Belorussian Front along the Küstrin bridgehead were substantially greater than those facing Konev's 1st Ukrainian Front along the Neisse bridgehead as summarized in the accompanying chart from the later Soviet General Staff study.

German 9. Armee strength, April 16, 1945

	Frontage	Troops	Mortars	Field guns	Tanks and AFV
Kustrin Bridgehead (Güstebiese–Podelzig)	44km	127,600	819	1,889	733
Neisse Bridgehead (Forst–Görlitz)	70km	66,100	457	701	245

Source: Military History Directorate, Soviet General Staff

German defensive tactics followed the lessons of 1918 and relied on "elastic defense." The forward edge of battle was lightly manned by an outpost line, followed by at least two more defense lines. The Red Army had already overrun the Ostwall fortified line on the old German–Polish border, so the new defense lines consisted mainly of earthen entrenchments reinforced by minefields and with pedestal antitank guns and Flak guns deployed in the direct fire role. As in the west, the eastern German cities were ringed with heavy Flak positions, and these substantially enhanced the army's field artillery. Behind these was any available mobile reserve for counterattacks.

Due to the obvious importance of the Küstrin–Seelow–Berlin axis, it was reinforced with no fewer than five defense lines along the main Reichsstrasse 1 highway to Berlin. The outpost line followed the German–Soviet front line and above this was the HKL (*Hauptkampflinie*: main defense line), about 5–6km behind the outpost line along the edge of the Seelow Heights. This

The battle for the Seelow Heights was complicated by the numerous canals, waterways and irrigation ditches in the Oderbruch marshland below the bluffs as seen in this contemporary tactical map.

actually consisted of two distinct lines, the Hardenburg-Stellung along the forward edge of the Seelow Heights and the Stein-Stellung behind the town. The 2. Stellung was about 4–5km behind the HKL, exploiting a series of wooded areas and reinforced by a number of flak batteries. The final defense line was the Wotan-Stellung, located 20–25km from the front line that was intended to prevent an operational breakout by Soviet tank forces. The main strongpoint on the Wotan-Stellung was the town of Müncheberg that sat astride the road to Berlin.

By this stage of the war, the Red Army was well aware of German elastic defense tactics. The usual Soviet tactic was to conduct a few days of vigorous reconnaissance-in-force to overwhelm the German outpost line and to disrupt German defensive preparations. So, the 1st Belorussian Front's artillery began pounding the area north and east of Küstrin starting on April 12 to suppress the German defenses in anticipation of the main attacks. The next stage of the battle began on April 14, 1945, with a short 15–20 minute artillery preparation followed by aggressive battalion-sized probes by the forward rifle divisions of the 1st Belorussian and 1st Ukrainian Fronts. Due to the likelihood of high casualties in the probes along Reichstrasse 1 from Küstrin to the Seelow Heights, Chuikov's 8th Guards Army sacrificed penal companies to clear the Soviet and German minefields, followed by regular infantry units once penetrations were made. The reconnaissance raids continued for two days. Preparatory bombardment for the main assault began on the evening of April 15 when the 4th and 16th Air Armies began bombing and strafing the German defense lines.

The Heeresgruppe Weichsel commander, Gotthard Heinrici, was a seasoned veteran of the Russian Front and had anticipated the Soviet tactics. As a result, on the evening of April 15, he ordered the majority of defenders in the outpost line to withdraw back to avoid the anticipated Soviet pre-assault artillery barrage.

German operational Panzer strength on the Berlin Front, April 10, 1945

	HG Mitte	HG Weichsel	Total
Pzkpfw III	3	2	5
PzKpfw IV	71	102	173
Pz IV/70	113	10	123
Panther	116	83	199
Tiger	1	46	47
Stug III	215	202	417
Stug IV	29	20	49
StuH	15	38	53
JagdPz 38	198	187	385
Nashorn	39	0	39
Jagdpanther	5	0	5
Total	805	690	1,495

THE BATTLE FOR THE SEELOW HEIGHTS

Zhukov's attack began in the pre-dawn hours of April 16 with a short but furious 30-minute artillery strike to a depth of 10–12km. One innovation in the attack was the use of searchlights to blind the German troops and illuminate their positions. However, the artillery bombardment smothered the battlefield with dust and smoke, and the searchlight illumination served as much to confuse the Soviet troops as the Germans.

The main Soviet attack along the Küstrin–Berlin highway was conducted by Gen. Nikolai Berzarin's 5th Shock Army on the north side and Gen. Vasili Chuikov's 8th Guards Army on the south side. The 5th Shock Army had five rifle divisions in the initial attack, staggered in two echelons. They were faced by one regiment of the 309. Infanterie-Division and two regiments of the 9. Fallschirmjäger-Division. The 8th Guards Army had three rifle corps, each with two rifle divisions in the first echelon and one in the second. They were opposed by the 303. Infanterie-Division and elements of the

There was fierce fighting in the Oder bridgehead at Küstrin in the weeks before the Berlin offensive. This is a Panther Ausf. G, probably from Pz.Rgt. 29 of Panzer-Division "Müncheberg," knocked out along the Kietz–Golzow road on March 27–28, 1945 during the second and final attempt to relieve the Festung Küstrin garrison. (Viktor Kulikov)

GERMAN UNITS

9. Armee
LVI. Panzer-Korps
A. s.Pz.Abt. 502
   309. Infanterie Division
B. I./Grenadier-Regiment. 652
   9. Fallschirmjäger-Division
C. Fallschirmjäger-Rgt. 25
D. Fallschirmjäger-Rgt. 26
E. Fallschirmjäger-Rgt. 27
   Panzer-Division "Müncheberg"
F. I./PzGrRgt. 2 "Müncheberg"
G. III./PzGrRgt. 2 "Müncheberg"
H. I./Pz.Rgt. "Müncheberg"

20. Panzergrenadier-Division
I. Panzergrenadier-Regiment. 76
J. Panzergrenadier-Regiment. 90
   303. Infanterie-Division
K. Grenadier-Regiment. 300
L. Grenadier-Regiment. 301
M. Grenadier-Regiment. 302
N. 18. Panzergrenadier-Division
German defense lines
O. Hardenberg Stellung
P. Stein Stellung
Q. 2. Stellung

▼ EVENTS

April 16

1 Soviet artillery preparation by army and corps units begins at 0300hrs with ten minutes against front-line positions, and 10–12 minutes of counter-battery fire. Divisional artillery opens fire around 0310hrs and the peak intensity of the barrage is reached at 0325hrs. Soviet infantry attack begins around 0320hrs.

2 After pushing past the I./GR. 652 of the 309. Infanterie-Division south of Letshchin, the 26th Guards Rifle Corps is stymied by defenses along the Haupt Grabben Canal through April 16. Only a single bridge is available about a kilometer west of Letschin, which is the scene of fierce fighting.

3 The advance by the 32nd Guards Rifle Corps is hit by a counterattack of the II./FS-Rgt. 25 supported by tanks around 0600hrs. The corps eventually pushes to the train embankment past Buschdorf.

4 The 9th Rifle Corps reaches the railway junction near Alt Langsow and Werbig. The area is heavily defended by FS-Rgt. 26 and elements of PzGrRgt. 2 "Muncheberg," as well as Flak train "Berlin" armed with 88mm guns running along the Seelow Heights

5 In the 8th Guards Army sector, the rifle divisions are stymied by the Haupt Grabben Canal. On becoming trapped in front of the canal, the supporting 105th and 106th Heavy Tank Regiments lose 16 IS-2 heavy tanks to Panther tanks of the I./Pz.Rgt. "Müncheberg" and 88mm Flak guns on the heights above.

6 At 1600hrs, the second echelon rifle divisions of the 8th Guards Army are committed, and finally get troops over the Haupt Grabben Canal to the edge of the bluffs in front of Seelow, encountering troops of the FS-Rgt. 27, 9. Fallschirmjäger-Division. A few SU-76M assault guns arrive at the foot of the bluffs, but are unable to advance up the steep slopes.

7 By the evening of April 16, the 57th Guards Rifle Division reaches the road between Seelow and Gusow.

8 The 27th Guards Rifle Division gets on top of the Seelow Heights near Friedersdorf, but is halted by a demolished railroad bridge over a ravine.

9 The 79th Guards Rifle Division captures Sachsendorf and reaches Dolgelin around 1400hrs. The town houses the headquarters of the 303. Infanterie-Division, and the divisional commander is seriously wounded. German tank reinforcements arrive, including six Kingtiger tanks of s.Pz.Abt. 502.

10 Around noon on April 16, the three corps of the 2nd Guards Tank Army begin moving forward through Gorgast. Elements of the 9th Guards Tank corps take part in the fighting around Letschin in the late afternoon.

11 Elements of the 11th Tank Corps reach Werbig at the foot of the bluff north of Seelow.

12 Lead elements of the 1st Guards Tank Army begin moving forward around noon. The 11th Guards Tank Corps attempts push into Seelow from the south.

13 The 8th Guards Mechanized Corps enters the fight in the afternoon for the railway stations including Dogelin.

April 17

14 The 301st Rifle Division, 9th Rifle Corps, finds Gusow too heavily fortified, but in cooperation with the second echelon 248th Rifle Division, they bypass the town and take it from the rear.

15 With tank support from the 1st Mechanized Corps, Platkow is taken later in the afternoon. This puts the 5th Shock Army over the Alte Oder River.

16 The 219th Tank Brigade, 1st Mechanized Corps, takes the town of Wulkow later in the evening.

17 The mission for the 2nd Guards Tank Army on April 17 is to make a passage over the Alte Oder River and numerous other water obstacles in their sector. The 9th Guards Tank Corps reaches the western banks near Friedland.

18 The 12th Guards Tank Corps crosses west of Quappendorf.

19 The 1st Mechanized Corps crosses the water barriers west of Platkow. The day is spent defending the bridgeheads to permit engineers to construct bridging.

20 The 11th Tank Corps along with the 35th Guards Rifle Division continues to press to the southwest over the Fliess stream. They are eventually halted when approaching the Muncheberg–Seelow highway due to the presence of four Luftwaffe Flak regiments and arriving elements of the 18. Panzergrenadier-Division.

21 The 11th Guards Tank Corps takes the town of Friedersdorf on the heights south of Seelow in the late morning of April 17, supported by the 35th and 47th Guards Rifle Divisions of the 4th Guards Rifle Corps. They are unable to push further forward due to heavy German artillery and antitank fire.

22 The 57th Guards Rifle Division around 1300hrs on April 17 pushes over the Seelow Heights and the Fliess stream, capturing the town of Seelow. The division then captures the villages of Görtsdorf to the west.

BREAKTHROUGH ON THE SEELOW HEIGHTS
April 16–17, 1945

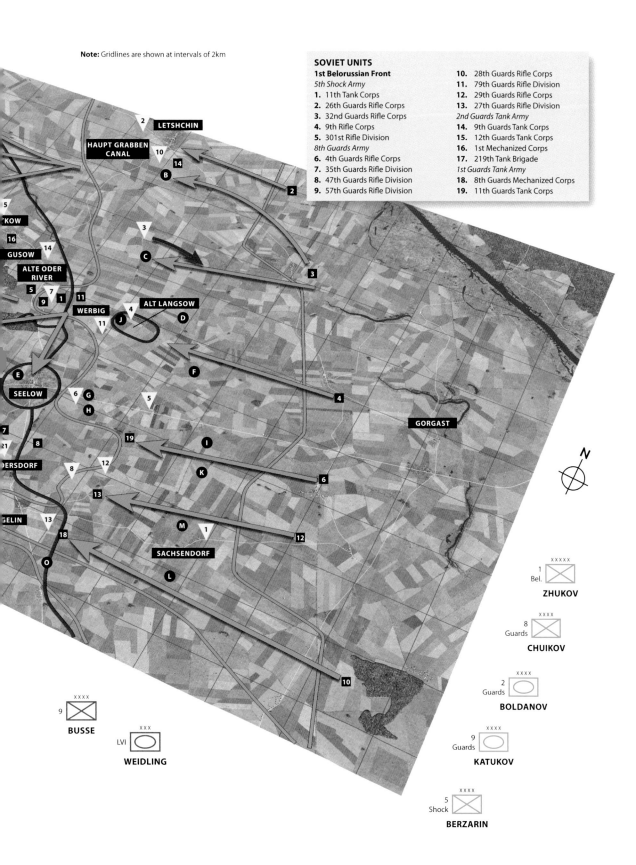

The attack on the Seelow Heights began with a short but intense artillery preparation in the pre-dawn hours. This is a pair of 203mm B-4 heavy howitzers.

20. Panzergrenadier-Division and Panzer-Division "Müncheberg." The Soviet rifle divisions were supported by heavy tank regiments with IS-2 tanks and assault gun regiments with SU-76 and ISU-152 assault guns.

The Seelow battlefield was dominated by two terrain features. The foreground was the Oderbruch (Oder Marsh), a swampy area of farm fields to the west of the Oder River, inundated by spring rains, and crisscrossed with streams and canals. Near the base of the bluffs was the Haupt Grabben Canal which merged with the Alte Oder River further north in the 5th Shock Army sector. Overlooking the Oderbruch was the Seelower Höhen (Seelow Heights). These bluffs were not especially high at 50–60m, but they dominated the flat Oderbruch and they were steep enough to prevent access by tanks except for a few well-guarded ravines. Adding to the complications were German minefields as well as Soviet minefields that had not been cleared prior to the start of the attack.

The Soviet infantry assault was painfully slow due to the terrain difficulties and the German resistance. Progress was especially difficult in Chuikov's 8th Guards Army sector due to the exposure of troops to German artillery that was accurately directed by observers on the top of the bluffs. Even after crossing the Oderbruch, the infantry was stymied by the Haupt Grabben Canal at the base of the Seelow Heights. Most bridges over the canal had been demolished and the one surviving bridge was under intense German artillery fire. It took time for Soviet engineers to create crossings over the canal. Around noon, Zhukov visited Chuikov's headquarters and, in a tense meeting, castigated him for the delays in seizing the Seelow Heights. Chuikov was intending to launch a coordinated assault two hours later. Irate and impatient, Zhukov decided instead to commit his exploitation force, the 2nd Guards Tank Army in Berzarin's sector and the 1st Guards Tank Army in Chuikov's sector. There was already ample tank support in both sectors, but the armor had proven ineffective due to the mud, mines, and fortified villages. Committing the exploitation force so early violated prudent tactical practice.

The lead tank brigades arrived in the Oderbruch in the late afternoon. Movement to the front was severely hampered by the congestion in the Küstrin bridgehead and the lack of passable routes over the muddy marshland. By midnight, Chuikov's infantry had won a small toehold on the edges of the town of Seelow, but his army was still far short of the plan's objective. Armored vehicle losses on the first day of the offensive in Chuikov's 8th Guards Army included 55 IS-2s, 22 T-34s, six ISU-152s, and 47 SU-76Ms; of these, 36 were from the 1st Guards Tank Army but most were from the independent regiments supporting the rifle divisions.

The situation was much the same in Berzarin's 5th Shock Army. The rifle divisions in the north secured the town of Letschin, but had not crossed the Alte Oder River. The forces on the left flank fought a series of vicious skirmishes along the rail line from Langsow, but finally forced their way into Gusow and Werbig, where the Seelow Heights curb back towards the west. Casualties for the day in this army were 1,667: 369 killed and 1,298 wounded.

The forward command post of the 8th Guards Army on the approaches to Seelow Heights. From left to right are the army commander, Gen. Col. V. I. Chuikov, representative of the of the 1st Belorussian Front Gen. Lt. K. F. Telegin, and the front artillery commander, Gen. Lt. V. I. Kazakov.

In a tense telephone conversation with Stalin late that night, Zhukov rationalized the day's failures by claiming that it was better to destroy the German forces in open battle than confront them on the streets of Berlin in the coming days. Zhukov promised that the Seelow Heights would be in Soviet hands by the following evening.

Busse's 9. Armee had succeeded in halting the Soviet attack on the main axis for the first day. The army claimed to have knocked out 211 Soviet tanks in their sector. Nevertheless, the scale of the Soviet attack was very alarming and both the 303. Infanterie-Division and 9. Fallschimjäger-Division had suffered crippling casualties. Heeresgruppe Weichsel dug into its meager reserves and dispatched the 18. Panzergrenadier-Division and 25. Panzergrenadier-Division to Müncheberg to reinforce the Wotan-Stellung.

On the morning of April 17, Chuikov's 8th Guards Army enjoyed an early success in pushing through Gusow to the north of Seelow. The day's advance, though far from spectacular, led to penetrations north and south of Seelow. By noon, Soviet tanks had surmounted the Seelow Heights at Friedersdorf and Dolgelin and became mixed up in a struggle with elements of the Kurmark Division. A *Kampfgruppe* of the 23. SS- Panzergrenadier-Division "Nederland" and Panzerjagd-Brigade Dora attacked up the road from Diedersdorf towards Seelow but these were beaten back and Diedersdorf was taken by the 29th Guards Corps. The 57th Guards Rifle Division and tanks of the 11th Tank Corps entered Seelow by early afternoon.

By the afternoon of April 17, Berzarin's 5th Shock Army managed to punch through the HKL in the Oderbruch east of Neuhardenberg and then made inroads into the 2. Stellung facing Obersdorf. This put the 2nd Guards Tank Army overlooking the Seelow–Berlin road, but the approach to Berlin through this sector was through woods and hills that were hardly ideal for large-scale armored exploitation.

After two days of fighting, Zhukov's forces had reached the objectives they had planned to attain on the first day of the offensive. Busse's 9. Armee had survived another day of attacks, and both the 18. and 25. Panzergrenadier-Divisionen had begun to arrive as reinforcements. However, the HKL had

ATTACK ON THE SEELOW HEIGHTS, APRIL 16, 1945 (PP. 54–55)

The attacks by the Soviet rifle divisions on the morning of April 16, 1945 were heavily supported by armored vehicles (**1**). Each rifle corps usually had an attached tank regiment or brigade, and one or more assault gun regiments. Berzarin's 5th Shock Army had 324 tanks and assault guns; Chuikov's had 216 tanks and assault guns plus a special engineer tank regiment with 43 flamethrower and mine-roller tanks. So, for example, the 79th Guards Rifle Division on the left wing of the 8th Guards Army was supported by T-34 tanks of the 259th Separate Tank Regiment and IS-2 heavy tanks of the 34th Guards Heavy Tank Regiment. The armor tended to be concentrated in the first assault waves and there were about 30–40 armored vehicles per kilometer of front.

The use of this armor proved to be extremely difficult due to the soggy ground conditions in the Oderbruch area, not only due to mud, but also due to the numerous irrigation ditches that crisscrossed the landscape. As a result, the armored units often tried using the many small roads in the Oderbruch, but antitank guns in the towns often covered these. The dependence of the supporting armor on the roads inevitably led to clashes in the villages and towns in the approaches to the Seelow Heights (**2**). The towns were the focal points of German infantry defenses in the Oderbruch, and the German infantry at this stage of the war was amply provided with Panzerfaust antitank rocket launchers for dealing with Soviet tanks at close range.

The Soviet rifle regiments tried to avoid using the roads since these areas attracted the heaviest German fire (**3**). However, crossing the numerous farm fields was also costly since the German defenses included two Volks-Artillerie-Korps, with forwards observers located along the edge of the bluffs overlooking the Oderbruch. As a result, German artillery fire against the Soviet infantry tended to be both accurate and intense. Soviet rifle regiment commanders had been briefed to avoid protracted engagements in the towns and villages, and to bypass them and leave their reduction to subsequent waves. However, the terrain restrictions channelized the traffic through the villages, and the Soviet advance slowed down when local rifle regiment commanders felt obliged to clear the towns and villages.

been thoroughly penetrated during the course of the day's fighting as well as parts of the 2. Stellung, and there was ample evidence that several of the frontline divisions were disintegrating.

The 9. Armee defenses finally cracked on April 18, particularly in Chuikov's sector south of Seelow. Gen. Heinrici, the Heeresgruppe Weichsel commander, later admitted that "after days of heavy fighting, their resistance came to an end." Earlier, he had argued with the OKW that HG Weichsel should withdraw to the northwest of Berlin and avoid a fight for the city. The direction of the Soviet penetrations now made this option impossible.

On April 19, Chuikov first tasted the possibility of breakout when the 11th Guards Tank Corps managed to infiltrate the Wotan-Stellung defenses near Müncheberg. By this stage, Panzer-Division "Müncheberg" had created a defensive belt west of the city using the remnants of forces pulling back from the Seelow Heights. By evening, Chuikov's attack had shifted to the southern flank of the German defenses, with two tank brigades and most of the 27th Guards Rifle Division reaching Schönfelde by nightfall. Soviet infantry captured Müncheberg after dark. This day was one of the costliest for Chuikov's 8th Guards Army, but the penetration of the Wotan-Stellung broke the outer ring of Berlin defenses and the 1st Belorussian Front was only 25km from Berlin.

Having pushed past the German defenses on the Seelow Heights, a tank column of Zhukov's 1st Belorussian front advances down the Reichstrasse 1 highway between Küstrin and Berlin. The T-34-85 tank at the rear of the column is loaded with boxes of 85mm tank gun ammunition, anticipating the fighting ahead.

Soviet tank and AFV casualties, 1st Belorussian Front

	Destroyed	Knocked out	Other	Total
14 April	31	29	29	89
15 April	15	10	9	34
16 April	71	77	40	195
17 April	79	85	15	179
18 April	65	86	13	164
19 April	105	76	8	189
20 April	83	81	5	169
Total	449	444	119	1,012

FORCING THE NEISSE RIVER

Konev's 1st Ukrainian Front faced far different problems than Zhukov's forces since they had to conduct a contested crossing of the Neisse River. The offensive was launched south of the fortified city of Frankfurt-an-der-Oder and on either side of Cottbus using three field armies: the 3rd Guards Army, 13th Army, and 5th Guards Army. Two further field armies, the Polish 2nd Army and the 52nd Army, were assigned to conduct a separate crossing operation towards Dresden that was part of the deception plan hinting at a more southerly focus. The German defenses in this sector followed the usual practice, with the outpost line located on the west bank of the Neisse River, the second Matilda-Stellung about 10km to the west, and the third line along the Spree River.

The Neisse River was 40–50m wide in this sector, so an orchestrated engineer effort was conducted with extensive artillery support. The artillery preparation began before dawn on April 16 with a special emphasis on counter-battery fire and smoke laying. The bombardment lasted 40 minutes and the smoke laying operation proved very successful, obscuring the river valley. The engineers brought forward about 2,440 assault boats for the first-wave assault battalions, quickly followed by assault bridges. Of the 150 intended crossing sites, the Red Army secured 133. By noon, the heavy 60-ton bridges were deployed to permit the passage of the tank armies. The first large-scale tank deployment over the river began in the 5th Guards Army sector in the early afternoon.

Konev's forces penetrated the first defense line of the 4. Panzer-Armee, and parts of the Matilda-Stellung by evening, to a depth of about 10km in some sectors. German defenses on this front consisted primarily of understrength infantry divisions supported by a modest armored force that included the 21. Panzer-Division and the Führer-Begleit-Division. The excellent progress of the bridging operation, as well as the penetration of the German defense lines, led to the commitment of the 3rd and 4th Guards Tank Armies on the evening of April 16. The collapse of the German defenses in this sector forced Heeresgruppe Mitte to commit not only their tactical reserves but also their operational reserves including their meager Panzer forces. The 10. SS-Panzer-Division was sent to reinforce the Matilda-Stellung around Spremburg.

Konev kept up the pressure through the night of April 16–17 with the aim of thoroughly overcoming the Matilda-Stellung the following day. The attacks on April 17 pushed the 1st Ukrainian Front over the Spree River. The river was not especially wide, and the 3rd Guards Tank Army located enough fords that engineer bridging operations were not necessary. In one of the few significant tank engagements in this sector, the 54th Guards Tank Brigade engaged the 21. Panzer-

An ISU-122 assault gun of the Polish 25th Self-propelled Gun Regiment, 1st Armored Corps crosses the Neisse river over an engineer bridge at the start of the offensive.

Advance on Berlin, April 16–25, 1945

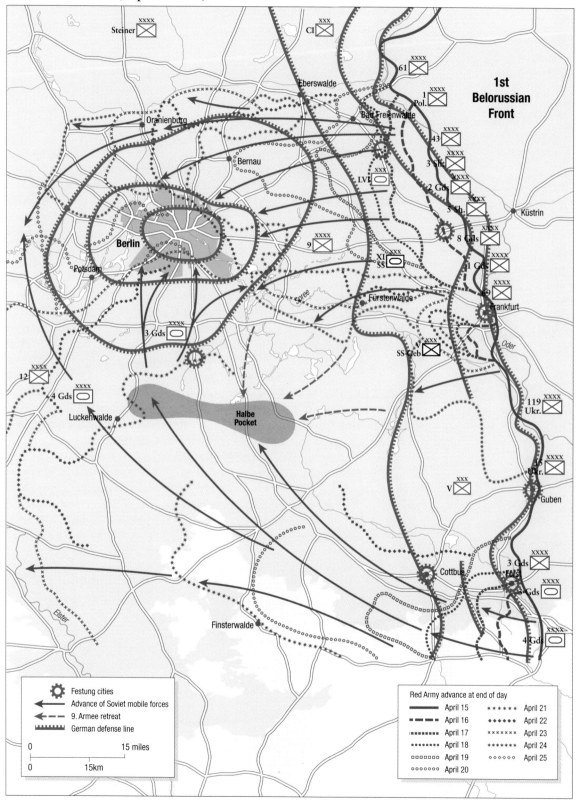

Steiner | CI
1st Belorussian Front
Eberswalde
Oranienburg | Bad Freienwalde
61
1 Pol.
43
3 Sh.
2 Gds
5 Sh.
Küstrin
8 Gds
1 Gds
69
Frankfurt
Bernau
LVL
9
XI SS
Berlin
Potsdam
Fürstenwalde
Spree
Oder
3 Gds
SS-Geb
12
4 Gds
Luckenwalde
Halbe Pocket
119 Ukr.
V
15 Ukr.
Guben
Elster
Cottbus
3 Gds Fors
5 Gds
Finsterwalde
4 Gds

Festung cities
Advance of Soviet mobile forces
9. Armee retreat
German defense line

| 0 | 15 miles |
| 0 | 15km |

Red Army advance at end of day

	April 15	******	April 21
---	April 16	◆◆◆◆◆	April 22
	April 17	×××××××	April 23
••••••	April 18	*******	April 24
□□□□□□	April 19	◇◇◇◇◇	April 25
○○○○○○	April 20		

Division around Mattendorf and Gahry starting in the late morning. This division was the strongest German formation in this sector, with 64 tanks and 48 tank destroyers and assault guns. After the encounters, the division was forced to withdraw over the Spree.

The success of Konev's attacks on April 17 forced the 4. Panzer-Armee to order a withdrawal to the third defense line along the Spree River. General Gräser, the 4. Panzer-Armee commander, presumed that the Red Army would need the Spree bridges near Cottbus and Spremberg on either flank of the Soviet penetration, and so focused his defenses on these locations with the 21. Panzer-Division anchoring the Cottbus defenses and the newly arrived 10. SS-Panzer-Division at Spremberg. In fact, 3rd Guards Tank Army was already over the Spree, and, after some difficulties further south, 4th Guards Tank Army followed over the same fords. Both tank armies had retained substantial tactical bridging to deal with the Spree, and so the fords were soon joined with additional river crossing sites erected by the Soviet engineers.

Berlin had a poor appreciation for the depth of the penetration south of Cottbus and Hitler ordered GFM Schörner to prepare a counteroffensive from the Görlitz area on the south side of the penetration. The OKH amplified the plan by ordering a concurrent attack by Busse's 9. Armee from the north, a preposterous idea given its precarious grasp of the Seelow Heights.

Konev's progress was so promising that Stalin suggested that Zhukov's two tank armies should be redeployed into Konev's sector. Konev discouraged the idea, arguing that such a movement would take too much time and that his forces were sufficient for the mission. Stalin was confident enough in Konev's judgment that he authorized a major change in plans. The original objectives for the 1st Ukrainian Front had been well south of Berlin, with the city entirely in Zhukov's sector. In view of the new conditions, Stalin changed the front boundaries and instructed Konev to aim his two tank armies against the southern approaches to Berlin. In the early morning hours of April 18, Konev issued orders to the 3rd and 4th Tank Armies, stressing that speed was of the essence and that they were to avoid being tied down by German strongpoints. Rybalko's 3rd Guards Tank Army was the star performer. The OKW hastily formed the Division Jahn using RAD teenagers, and deployed it south of Berlin under the exaggerated title of Armeegruppe Spree. Konev's tank units overran it before it fully deployed.

An old Panther Ausf. D tank of Panzergrenadier-Division "Brandenburg" knocked out by an IS-2m of the Polish 5th Heavy Tank Regiment during the fighting near Rothenburg/ Oberlausitz shortly after the Neisse River crossing on the night of April 16–17.

NORTH OF BERLIN

Rokossovskiy's 2nd Belorussian Front finally began its attack in the pre-dawn hours of April 20 after two days of preliminary reconnaissance probes. The water obstacles in this sector were especially challenging as the Oder north of Schwedt bifurcated into a western and eastern branch, with shifting marshes and sandbars in between.

Batov's 65th Army formed the northern element of the attack on the southern outskirts of the port of Stettin. The assault used small boats and there were no bridges erected until early afternoon. Nevertheless, a firm bridgehead was established, even in the face of repeated artillery attacks from nearby Stettin. Popov's 70th Army in the center made a similar river crossing, but became badly entangled in a series of dikes and canals on the western bank of the Oder, only managing to gain a small foothold. The only river assault to fail on April 20 was Grishin's 49th Army, attacking on the northern flank of the 1st Belorussian Front. The plans had confused the various waterways, and by day's end, there were only small detachments on the western side of the Oder.

Batov's forces were counterattacked by the 27. Langemark-Division and the 281. Infanterie-Division but managed to hold their ground. Rokossovskiy decided to reinforce success and pushed additional engineer equipment into Batov's sector to add heavy bridges and reinforce the bridgehead defenses with armor and artillery. This front lacked a tank army, and so its progress was far slower than Zhukov's and Konev's.

THE RACE FOR BERLIN

Stalin's change of plans on the afternoon of April 17 initiated the race for Berlin. Stalin was well aware of the rivalry between Konev and Zhukov, and expected that the competition would lead to a swifter and bolder campaign. Konev's progress by April 18, along with the start of Rokossovskiy's offensive, threatened to envelop the 9. Armee.

By Hitler's birthday, April 20, the Soviet spearheads had reached the outer approaches of Berlin. The city was subjected to its last heavy bombing by British and American bombers, and Zhukov's artillery finally came in range of the eastern suburbs of the capitol. Konev's forces raced from the south with the 3rd Guard Tank Army in the vanguard. Late in the day, both Konev and Zhukov sent orders to the lead elements of their tank armies, encouraging them to rush select tank brigades into the streets of Berlin to claim the honor of being the first Soviet troops to reach Hitler's lair. In reality, the bulk of both fronts were still a few days' march from Berlin.

Hitler dithered over whether to withdraw the 9. Armee back towards Berlin to assist in the final defense or order them to strike exposed Soviet flanks from their current locations. In reality, neither HG Mitte nor HG Weichsel had sufficient resources to stem the Soviet advance, and HG Weichsel was at risk of losing large chunks of the 9. Armee to encirclement due to the rapid pace of the Soviet advance. HG Weichsel became split in two, with 3. Panzer-Armee to the northeast of Berlin, and 9. Armee trapped in a pocket to the southeast.

ROBOT FLYING BOMBS OVER THE ODER, APRIL 1945 (PP. 62–63)

In a desperate move to sever the Red Army's logistical links over the Oder River, Hitler ordered an all-out Luftwaffe assault to destroy the Oder bridges. The chosen weapon was the Mistel, one of Germany's more obscure secret weapons. First called the "Beethoven Gerät," the Mistel consisted of a war-weary Ju-88G night fighter converted into a flying bomb with an Fw-190 fighter attached above to guide it to the target area (**1**). The Ju-88 had its normal cockpit removed and replaced with a massive 3.8-ton shaped-charge warhead fitted with an *Elefantrüssel* (Elephant tusk) detonation probe on front. Both aircraft were controlled by the Fw-190 above, and once the target area was reached, the pilot activated the Mistel's autopilot and then aimed it at the target using a special reflex sight. About 1,000m from the target, the pilot triggered the separation system, which detonated small explosive charges to break the link between the two aircraft. The Mistel flying bomb then flew into the target on automatic pilot while the Fw-190 escaped (**2**).

The Mistel was originally assigned to strike at the Royal Navy warships in Scapa Flow, and its shaped-charge warhead could penetrate up to 26ft of steel armor. Allied intelligence spotted the early deployments in April 1944, and made relentless air attacks on their home bases. After the D-Day landings, the mission of the Mistel changed, including a failed attack on the Allied fleet off Normandy on June 14, 1944, and the stillborn Operation *Eisenhammer*, a plan to strike vital Soviet powerplants in the Moscow and Gorkiy area. Following the Vistula–Oder offensive in January 1945, the plan switched again, with the new objective being the bridges over the Vistula near Warsaw. Many of the Mistel assembled for the attack were destroyed on the ground by Allied air attacks. In March 1945, Hitler ordered Oberstleutnant Walter Baumbach, commander of KG 200, to prepare the Mistels for attacks on the Oder River bridges. The first attack on March 8, 1945 narrowly missed the bridge at Göritz. There were small-scale attacks on other Oder bridges over the next few weeks, as well as a failed attempt to hit the Rhine crossing sites of Patton's Third US Army near Oppenheim on the night of March 25. The first successful mission was conducted on March 31 with two impacts on the Oder bridge at Steinau. The focus of the attacks in early April shifted to the bridges near Küstrin. German troops observing the attacks from the Seelow Heights dubbed them as "Vater und Sohn" (father and son).

As seen in the illustration here, the usual tactic was to stage an attack with four or more Mistel (**3**). Ju-188 bombers usually served as the pathfinders for the group and also conducted attacks on Soviet anti-aircraft gun positions with cluster bombs. The Mistel never proved very effective due to the high loss rate to roving Allied fighters and antiaircraft guns as well as the mechanical unreliability of the combination.

Command of the German field armies was crippled on April 21, when the 6th Tank Corps smashed into Zossen and captured the massive fortified headquarters of the OKW. The senior staff had already been evacuated the evening before the Soviet arrival, but the capture of the headquarters complex was a severe blow to German command-and-control since it was at the center of the army's communication network. National command was split in two, with a new OKW Führungsgruppe B under Gen. August Winter sent to the Berchtesgarden area in southern Germany while the rump OKW moved about the Berlin area for a few days before eventually escaping to Flensburg in northern Germany in early May. The bifurcation of the headquarters was due to the recognition that the Wehrmacht in Germany was on the verge of being split into northern and southern sectors.

Konev's and Zhukov's forces now faced two distinctly different opponents – the Berlin defenses in front of them and bypassed forces behind them. The rapidity of the advance had left a sizeable number of German troops in pockets to the rear, several of which such as Gruppe Cottbus posed a significant threat. The 9. Armee was in headlong retreat, ending up trapped between Zhukov's and Konev's forces in the forested Halbe pocket south of Berlin.

Additional units of both fronts reached the outskirts of Berlin late on April 21. Zhukov planned to conduct his attack from the run, with special street-fighting assault groups already organized. Three armies – the 2nd Guards Tank Army, 3rd Shock Army, and 47th Army – formed the right wing of Zhukov's assault against the northeastern side of Berlin while three other armies – the 1st Guards Tank Army, 5th Shock Army, and 8th Guards Army – formed the left wing of the attack from the southeast and east. Konev's assault began with probes by the 3rd Tank Army in the southern suburbs, but the main assault had to wait until the slower moving armies caught up. In spite of Zhukov's and Konev's prodding late on April 20, the spearheads of the two fronts could not push deep into the city until April 22.

The three Berlin Flak tower complexes incorporated large civil defense shelters that could hold thousands of civilians. This is the gun tower in the Tiergarten near the Berlin zoo. The entrances had been reinforced before the attack to withstand ground assault. This tower withstood the heaviest Soviet field artillery and did not surrender until after the capitulation of the city defenses.

THE BERLIN DEFENSES

In February 1945, Hitler declared Berlin to be a "Festung" (fortress) to be defended to the last man. The commander of Verteidigungsbereich Berlin (Berlin Defense Zone), Gen.Lt. Hellmuth Reymann, had a modest security garrison in the city of about 60,000 Volkssturm troops in 92 battalions. They were poorly armed and trained and nearly a third had no weapons at all. Reymann organized a construction program by about 70,000 civilians to create defense positions and antitank obstacles in the city in the weeks before the final battle. One of the main sources for heavy weapons was the

As a means to quickly reinforce key street intersections in Berlin, tanks were collected from local repair depots and buried up to their turrets to create improvised strongpoints. This is an old Panther Ausf. D tank that was deployed at Sophie-Charlotten-Platz and played a significant role in fighting against the 2nd Guards Tank Army in this sector. (Viktor Kulikov)

Luftwaffe's Flak batteries, which had 249 20mm/37mm guns, 270 88mm guns and 72 105mm/128mm guns around the city.

The Berlin defenses were organized into a series of successive defense lines which a semi-official history of Festung Berlin later described as "pure fiction." The outer defense perimeter was 10km east of the city consisting of modest and incomplete blocking positions between the numerous lakes from the Tiefensee down to Königswusterhausen. The main city defenses consisted of four defense lines, starting with the 1. Stellung on the outskirts of the city, the 2. Stellung about 5km inside the outer barrier, and then two inner defense zones, delineated by the Ringbahn city rail lines and finally the Zitadelle (Citadel) defense zone within the Landwehr Canal and Spree River that contained most of the government buildings. The issue of bridge demolition was controversial. Some of the army commanders wanted the bridges knocked down to slow the Soviet advance. Reichsminister Speer, nominally in charge of the demolition effort, argued against too much demolition for fear of the post-war consequences. In the event, of Berlin's 248 bridges, some 120 were demolished and nine damaged. Likewise, the issue of flooding the subway tunnels was never resolved though the tunnel near the Landwehr Canal was flooded under obscure circumstances.

Even in these desperate circumstances, the command of the Berlin defenses became embroiled in political maneuvers between the army and the Nazi Party. Hitler assigned the defense of Festung Berlin to Heeresgruppe Weichsel on April 19, and Heinrici ordered Reymann to deploy all available forces from within the

Hitler's headquarters was located in the Reichskanzlei, the Reich Chancellery. This is a view from the Wilhelmstrasse side with the new Reich Chancellery in the left center, and the old Reich Chancellery to the left. The Führerbunker was located in the garden behind the old Reich Chancellery, roughly in the center of this photo (Library of Congress)

city to defensive positions along its eastern perimeter. Propaganda minister Joseph Goebbels appointed himself as the Reich Defense Commissar for Berlin. He was unhappy with Reymann and applied pressure to send him off to command the improvised Armeegruppe Spree. On April 22, Goebbels appointed Oberst Ernst Kaether, the head of Nazi Party indoctrination commissars, to lead the Berlin defenses. Heinrici ordered Reymann to remain at his post to avoid such a confusing change of command at a critical moment. Under these circumstances, only about 30 Volkssturm battalions were moved to the outer Berlin defenses – which was too little, too late.

Heinrici again requested permission to withdraw 9. Armee towards the city, but Hitler refused and on April 22 relieved Heinrici of any responsibility for the Berlin defenses. On April 22, he ordered LVI. Panzer-Korps, commanded by Gen. der Artillerie Helmuth Weidling, to withdraw back to Berlin to reinforce the meager city garrison. When Weidling was slow to get his forces moving, Hitler ordered him to report to the Führerbunker on pain of death. Instead of being shot, Weidling made such a favorable impression on Hitler that he was named commander of the Berlin defense zone. The city had eight defense sectors, labeled A through H, and he intended to have each of his four divisions responsible for two of the sectors. Weidling faced the usual aggravation of attempting to subordinate the Luftwaffe's 1. Flak-Division and the Waffen-SS government security brigade to his command. To further complicate the matter, Goebbels established a War Council to supervise the Berlin defenses.

Goebbels, as the RVK for Berlin, never paid any attention to the issue of evacuation of the civilian population. The city's usual population of 4.5 million had decreased to about 2.5 million by the end of 1944, but a wave of evacuations from the east increased the population to 3–3.5 million by April 1945. The army wanted a citywide evacuation which Goebbels refused to countenance.

Most of Weidling's LVI. Panzer-Korps arrived in Berlin on April 22–23, exploiting the vacuum between the 1st Belorussian and 1st Ukrainian Fronts. It consisted of the remnants of Panzer-Division "Müncheberg," the 18. and 20. Panzergrenadier-Divisionen, and SS- Panzergrenadier-Division "Nordland." The 20. Panzergrenadier-Division was especially weak, but the other three divisions still retained some combat capability. There were only about 50–60 functional tanks near the city. The 408. Volks-Artillerie-Korps had four light battalions and two heavy battalions, but very little ammunition. The Waffen-SS security detachments in the government sector were consolidated as a *Kampfgruppe* under SS- Brigadeführer Wilhelm Mohnke and assigned to defend the Zitadelle. The Berlin defenses totaled about 60,000 regular troops and another 90,000 in the Luftwaffe Flak regiments, Volkssturm and other assorted paramilitary forces. The Flak batteries proved to be one of the most valuable elements of the city defenses, but a semi-official history of the Berlin defenses categorized the value of the Volkssturm as "almost nil."

The Berlin police had an Ordnungspolizei armored car platoon equipped with obsolete vehicles that were deployed at the Reich Chancellery to transport important officials on the increasingly dangerous streets of the city. In the final days of the Berlin fighting, two of these were stationed in the Ehrenhof courtyard to guard the main entrance. The vehicle in the foreground is a 1921 Daimler DZVR Schupo-Sonderwagen and the one behind is a war-booty Dutch Wilton-Fijenoord Overvalwagen. (Viktor Kulikov)

Many heavy artillery weapons were brought into the streets of Berlin to help demolish German strongpoints. This is a BM-31-12, the heaviest and most powerful of the Katyusha multiple rocket launchers, that fired a dozen M-30 300mm rockets with 29kg warheads. (Viktor Kulikov)

THE BERLIN ASSAULT BEGINS

During a meeting in his bunker complex below the Reich Chancellery on April 22, Hitler's rage exploded. Instead of heading south to the Alpenfestung, he vowed to stay in Berlin: "Either I win the battle of Berlin or I die in Berlin." The leadership of Nazi Germany began to disintegrate. Göring, the heir apparent, sent a cable from Berchtesgarden enquiring whether Hitler's decision to stay in embattled Berlin meant that he should take over the government. Infuriated, Hitler ordered him arrested. Himmler had already left Berlin for northern Germany, and on learning of Hitler's April 22 emotional collapse, began a bizarre series of attempts to negotiate with the Allies.

The evaporation of German defenses to the east of Berlin prompted Hitler to look elsewhere for saviors. Wenck's 12. Armee, holding the line along the Elbe against the US Army, was instructed to ignore the Americans, turn around, and head for Berlin to cut off Konev's 1st Ukrainian Front south of Potsdam. SS-Obergruppenführer Felix Steiner was instructed to form a special *Armeegruppe* from elements of the 3. Panzer-Armee and III. SS-Panzer-Korps north of the city to strike at Zhukov's 1st Belorussian Front. In view of the weakness of German forces near Berlin, such schemes were entirely delusional. The only attack to have some success was a Panzer attack from Bautzen by Gräser's 4. Panzer-Armee that struck a gap between the 52nd Army and Polish 2nd Army near Spremberg. This briefly distracted Konev, but it was too far from Berlin to have any impact on the siege and it was checked by April 24.

The Red Army regarded the derelict Reichstag building as the symbol of Nazi power, even though it had not been used since the 1933 fire. As a result, there was a determined effort to capture the building. The 150th Rifle Division secured a foothold in the western side of the building on April 30, but it took more than a day's fighting to completely secure the building from Kampfgruppe Mohnke.

Zhukov used his mobile forces to begin the encirclement of Berlin on April 23, with the 7th Cavalry Corps swinging wide to the northwest on the right flank, and the 9th Guards Mechanized Corps sweeping closer to the city before heading along its western perimeter. On April 25, the 1st Belorussian Front and 1st Ukrainian Front completed the encirclement, meeting in the southwest suburbs of Berlin.

The encirclement of Berlin and an imminent juncture of Soviet and American forces on the Elbe meant that German defenses would be bifurcated north and south. This led to yet another round of German command reorganization, trying to reestablish some sort of coherent defense. Keitel had escaped north with the rump OKW and was charged with organizing the army's defense in the north. South of Berlin, GFM Kesselring was put in charge of all German forces including Bavaria, Austria, northern Italy, the Czech lands, and Yugoslavia.

A flight of IL-2 Shturmovik attack aircraft of the 567th Attack Aviation Regiment, 16th Air Army on a mission over Berlin in April 1945.

The street around the Friedrichstrasse railway station is littered with shattered equipment after a group under SS-Brigadefuhrer Gustav Kurkenberg made a costly attempt to try to escape Berlin over the neighboring Weidendamm Bridge on the night of May 1–2. This photo was taken on May 4, and the buildings are still smoldering. (NARA)

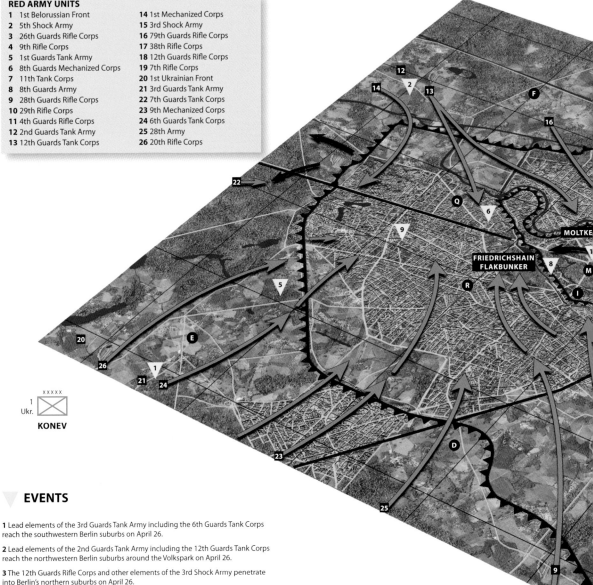

RED ARMY UNITS

1	1st Belorussian Front	**14**	1st Mechanized Corps
2	5th Shock Army	**15**	3rd Shock Army
3	26th Guards Rifle Corps	**16**	79th Guards Rifle Corps
4	9th Rifle Corps	**17**	38th Rifle Corps
5	1st Guards Tank Army	**18**	12th Guards Rifle Corps
6	8th Guards Mechanized Corps	**19**	7th Rifle Corps
7	11th Tank Corps	**20**	1st Ukrainian Front
8	8th Guards Army	**21**	3rd Guards Tank Army
9	28th Guards Rifle Corps	**22**	7th Guards Tank Corps
10	29th Rifle Corps	**23**	9th Mechanized Corps
11	4th Guards Rifle Corps	**24**	6th Guards Tank Corps
12	2nd Guards Tank Army	**25**	28th Army
13	12th Guards Tank Corps	**26**	20th Rifle Corps

xxxxx
1
Ukr.

KONEV

▼ EVENTS

1 Lead elements of the 3rd Guards Tank Army including the 6th Guards Tank Corps reach the southwestern Berlin suburbs on April 26.

2 Lead elements of the 2nd Guards Tank Army including the 12th Guards Tank Corps reach the northwestern Berlin suburbs around the Volkspark on April 26.

3 The 12th Guards Rifle Corps and other elements of the 3rd Shock Army penetrate into Berlin's northern suburbs on April 26.

4 The 26th Guards Rifle Corps and 32nd Rifle Corps of the 5th Shock Army have the deepest penetrations into Berlin on April 26, pushing down along the north bank of the Spree River along the train tracks and nearly reaching the Jannowitz-Brücke rail station.

5 The 3rd Guards Tank Army reaches the inner Berlin defense line along the rail lines on the southwest side of Berlin on April 28.

6 The 2nd Guards Tank Army penetrates the inner Berlin defense line on April 27–28, reaching the Spree River and the Zitadelle.

7 German defenses on the southeastern side of Berlin collapse on April 27–28 as the 1st Guards Tank Army pushes along the south bank of the Spree River to reach the southeastern side of the Zitadelle defenses.

8 Other elements of the 1st Guards Tank Army including the 8th Guards Mechanized Corps are the first Soviet units to breach the Zitadelle defenses on April 27–28, crossing the Landwehr Canal near the Wehrmacht headquarters to the west of the Potsdamer rail station.

9 Remnants of the LVI. Panzer-Korps continue to hold back the 3rd Guards Tank Army in the Charlottenburg suburbs well into May 1, trying to hold open a corridor along the railway line.

10 Hitler commits suicide in his bunker at 1550hrs on the afternoon of April 30.

11 The 207th Rifle Division crosses the Spree River on April 29, takes the Gestapo headquarters on April 30, and pushes into the Reichstag on May 1. After a bitter fight to clear the Reichstag, the 756th Rifle Regiment hoists the Red Flag on May 2.

12 The defenses of the Zitadelle begin to collapse on May 1 and in spite of the ceasefire orders, fighting continues in the center of the city well into May 2.

13 Various party officials try to break out of the city from the area around the Führerbunker, trying to reach the northern suburbs via the Weidendamm Bridge over the Spree. Casualties are extremely heavy, including Nazi Party leader Martin Bormann.

THE BATTLE FOR BERLIN

April 26–May 2 1945

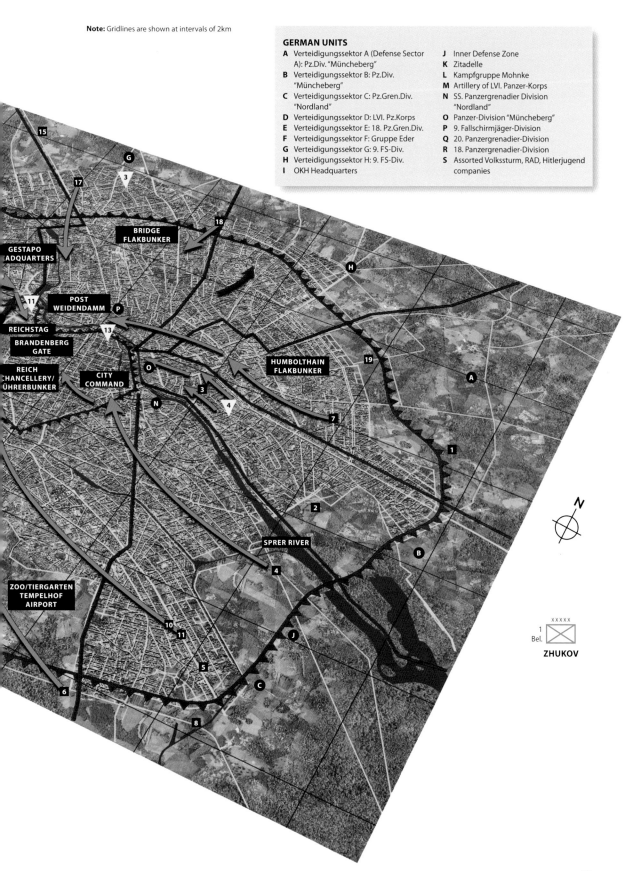

Note: Gridlines are shown at intervals of 2km

GERMAN UNITS

A Verteidigungssektor A (Defense Sector A): Pz.Div. "Müncheberg"
B Verteidigungssektor B: Pz.Div. "Müncheberg"
C Verteidigungssektor C: Pz.Gren.Div. "Nordland"
D Verteidigungssektor D: LVI. Pz.Korps
E Verteidigungssektor E: 18. Pz.Gren.Div.
F Verteidigungssektor F: Gruppe Eder
G Verteidigungssektor G: 9. FS-Div.
H Verteidigungssektor H: 9. FS-Div.
I OKH Headquarters

J Inner Defense Zone
K Zitadelle
L Kampfgruppe Mohnke
M Artillery of LVI. Panzer-Korps
N SS. Panzergrenadier Division "Nordland"
O Panzer-Division "Müncheberg"
P 9. Fallschirmjäger-Division
Q 20. Panzergrenadier-Division
R 18. Panzergrenadier-Division
S Assorted Volkssturm, RAD, Hitlerjugend companies

GESTAPO ADQUARTERS

BRIDGE FLAKBUNKER

POST WEIDENDAMM

REICHSTAG

BRANDENBERG GATE

REICH CHANCELLERY/ÜHRERBUNKER

CITY COMMAND

HUMBOLTHAIN FLAKBUNKER

SPRER RIVER

ZOO/TIERGARTEN TEMPELHOF AIRPORT

1
Bel.
ZHUKOV

OPPOSITE LEFT
During the Potsdam conference in July 1945, the new British foreign secretary, Ernest Bevin, was given a tour of the Reich Chancellery. This is the entrance to the Führerbunker in the chancellery gardens, and the bodies of Hitler and Eva Braun were burned in a trench slightly to the right of this image. (NARA)

OPPOSITE RIGHT
Germany deported millions of Soviet civilians for forced labor in factories and on farms back in the Reich. Here, on the outskirts of Berlin in May 1945, a Soviet cavalryman talks to a Soviet woman on her way back home.

BELOW
Red Army photographers staged a number of flag raising ceremonies around the city. The best known took place over the deserted Reichstag building, but this event took place near the Quadriga sculpture on top of the Brandenberg Gate. The Reichstag is evident in the background to the left. (Library of Congress)

Large German formations in eastern Germany began to face the prospect of falling into Soviet captivity should Berlin fall. Desperate battles began in the last week of April to break out westward, the intention being to reach American or British lines. The units trapped in Frankfurt-an-der-Oder began breakout attempts late on April 26, and Busse's 9. Armee continued to escape south of Berlin through the Halbe area.

By April 26, the Red Army was heavily engaged in street fighting inside Berlin. The Soviet tactics stressed firepower over manpower. There were ample numbers of tanks and assault guns to provide direct fire support, and both divisional and corps artillery were dragged into Berlin and used in a direct fire mode to reduce buildings. Even though the German defenders were grossly outnumbered, urban combat was a time-consuming and costly business. Soviet forces pushed into the Zitadelle sector of central Berlin on April 28 and it took three days of brutal fighting to secure the Tiergarten and Zoopark.

Hitler's health collapsed and by the final days of April, he finally admitted that the situation in Berlin had become hopeless. Word arrived that Himmler was attempting to negotiate a surrender; Hitler was shocked that even the SS had betrayed him. After fleeing Berlin, Heinrich Himmler approached the Swedish legation in Lübeck on April 23 as the "provisional leader of Germany" to negotiate surrender terms with Eisenhower. Before any agreement was reached, the BBC revealed these discussions during a radio broadcast on the evening of April 28. On hearing of this treachery, Hitler ordered Himmler's capture and execution.

Hitler also heard of Mussolini's grim fate in Italy on April 28 over the radio, and he became determined to avoid capture. On April 29, Weidling reported that the Berlin defenses were almost out of ammunition and there was no hope that any relief force would arrive. In the pre-dawn hours of April 30, Hitler was informed that neither Steiner nor Wenck's forces had any chance of relieving Berlin. In his final act, Hitler appointed Admiral Karl Dönitz as his successor and committed suicide in his bunker at 1550hrs on the afternoon of April 30. In the pre-dawn hours of May 1, Gen. Hans Krebs, the army chief-of-staff, made contact with Soviet forces in Berlin to inform them of Hitler's death and to begin negotiating for the surrender. The ceasefire did not come into effect in Berlin until 1500hrs on May 2 and fighting continued in isolated pockets around the city for several days.

Soviet casualties in the Berlin operation, April 16– May 8 1945

	KIA	Other	Total Casualties
1st Ukrainian Front	27,580	86,245	113,825
1st Belorussian Front	37,610	141,880	179,490
2nd Belorussian Front	13,070	46,040	59,110
1st and 2nd Polish Armies	2,825	6,067	8,892
Total	81,085	280,232	361,317

German casualties in the Berlin operation, April 16–May 9 1945*

	KIA	POW	Total Casualties
1st Ukrainian Front	189,619	144,530	334,149
1st Belorussian Front	218,691	250,534	469,225
2nd Belorussian Front	130,070	124,220	254,290
Total	538,380	519,284	1,057,664

*According to Soviet records; German records do not exist.

Following the fighting, officers and a tank crew pose on an IS-2m heavy tank of Col. Nikolai Yurenkov's 7th Ind. Guards Heavy Tank Regiment near the Brandenberg Gate. This unit had been supporting the rifle units during the attack on the Zitadelle in central Berlin.

LAST OF THE KINGTIGERS: BERLIN, MAY 1945 (PP. 74–75)

In late April 1945, a detachment of about a dozen Kingtiger heavy tanks from s.SS-Pz.Abt. 503 was committed to defend Berlin, starting with engagements on the Seelow Heights on April 16. About six to nine tanks survived the retreat to Berlin on April 24. The Kingtigers were usually deployed in small groups of two or three and often fought in the Zitadelle area in support of SS-Pz. Gren.Div. "Nordland". One group was active around the Potsdamer Bahnhof railroad station in the southeast corner of the Zitadelle, which offered good firing opportunities against Soviet tanks on the other side of the Landwehr Canal. The train stations had large plazas at the front which provided the Kingtiger tanks with excellent fields of fire. This area also served to block the approaches to the Führerbunker, which was a short distance north of the station. Hitler personally took note of the detachment's role in the Berlin defense, and decorated its commander, Obersturmbannführer Herzig with the Ritterkreuz at the Reich Chancellery on April 28.

The Kingtiger illustrated here, number 314 (**1**), was commanded by SS-Unterscharführer Georg Diers. On April 28, this tank and tank 100 commanded by SS-Oberscharführer Karl-Heinz Turk were ordered to stage an attack from the Postdamer station towards the Anhalter station several blocks to the southeast. They became engaged in a day-long melee with Soviet T-34-85 and IS-2 tanks. They were finally forced back to the Potsdamer station as seen here (**2**). On the morning of April 30, the Soviet tanks managed to penetrate further into the Zitadelle, and Turk's tank

was hit on the right front corner, ripping off the track and damaging the drive sprocket and final drive. On May 1, Turk's immobile Kingtiger was nearly overrun when a platoon of Soviet infantry suddenly appeared out of one of the sewer entrances; it was abandoned in the evening after running out of ammunition. Diers' crew claimed to have destroyed 39 Soviet tanks in the Berlin fighting.

Late in the day, after news of Hitler's death, a group of Nazi Party officials and Waffen-SS officers decided to break out from the Reich Chancellery area across the Weidendamm bridge towards Spandau in the north. All running tanks and half-tracks were assembled in the evening including Diers' Kingtiger. The escape attempt was led by SS-Brigadefuhrer Gustav Kurkenberg, mainly with troops of the SS-Pz. Gren.Div. "Nordland". The group set off around 2100hrs and was accompanied by many senior Nazi Party officials, including Martin Bormann. On reaching the Friedrichstrasse railway station, they came under continual fire from Soviet troops. Diers' Kingtiger moved over the Weidendamm bridge with many troops and civilians behind, but the Soviet troops had clear fields of fire from across the Spree River and it was a bloody slaughter. Diers' Kingtiger 314 reached the Humboldthain park with a small group of survivors, only to be disabled by a German mine.

At least two other Kingtigers were used in another breakout attempt to the southwest from the Charlottenburg district, but both were knocked out, one by a captured 88mm Flak gun.

THE JUNCTION OF ALLIED FORCES

Although the primary focus of Konev's 1st Ukrainian Front was Berlin, the 5th Guards Army on its southern flank made a brisk advance westward towards the Elbe River. There was little coordination between the Red Army and the US Army beyond the understanding that the Elbe represented the demarcation line. Although the Ninth US Army had been the first to reach the Elbe, their crossing sites were opposite Berlin. Leipzig was captured by the 69th Division of the First US Army on April 18–19, and Eilenberg on the Mulde River on April 23. The Red Army reached this sector of the Elbe on April 23 when a battalion of the 173rd Guards Rifle Regiment, 58th Guards Rifle Division, reached Torgau and set up a defense near one of the bridges. On April 25, the 2/273rd Infantry, 69th Division sent jeep patrols towards the Elbe. Soviet and American troops met near Strehla and Torgau in the late afternoon, and arranged for a more formal ceremony the following day between divisional commanders, followed by a meeting of higher commanders on April 27. The Elbe meeting was only the first of a string of encounters between US, British, and Soviet forces over the course of the following week.

After the first Soviet and American scout units met along the Elbe, senior officers began meeting for subsequent discussions. Here, the commander of the US V Corps, Maj. Gen. Clarence Huebner, heads over the Elbe on April 27 along with Col. Vladimir Rusakov, the commander of the 58th Guards Rifle Division, to hold discussions with the commander of the Red Army's 34th Guards Corps, Gen. Maj. Gleb Baklanov. (NARA)

A GI inspects a Soviet T-34-85 tank near Torgau, Germany on April 27, 1945 following the meetings along the Elbe River. (NARA)

THE NORTHERN GERMANY CAMPAIGN

Following the successful Operation *Plunder–Varsity* crossing of the Rhine in late March 1945, Montgomery's 21st Army Group proceeded to the northeast. On the left flank, the Canadian First Army was assigned to liberate the remainder of the Netherlands, an urgent task in view of the severe food shortages in the winter of 1944–45 and the widespread starvation among the Dutch. The British Second Army moved along towards Hamburg with an aim to rapidly capture the northern German plains.

Facing the 21st Army Group was Gen. Blaskowitz's Heeresgruppe H that had defended the North Sea coast since the summer campaign. It was gradually isolated in a coastal pocket west of the Zuider Zee. On April 6, 1945, the defense of northern Germany was reconfigured under the new Oberbefehlshaber Nordwest (OB Nordwest: Northwest high command) under GFM Ernst Busch and Heeresgruppe H was subordinated to it as OB-Niederlande. Aside from the two corps trapped in the Netherlands, the only other major formation in northwestern Germany was Student's 1. Fallschirm-Armee, with two corps. In the face of the British advance into Germany, Berlin tried to reinforce OB Nordwest with the new Armee-Blumentritt but this was a hollow formation made up of staffs and replacement units of neighboring military districts plus various improvised naval units from around the Bremen naval base.

The British advance was quite brisk, but there were numerous occasions when a significant German strongpoint would be encountered such as along the Dortmund–Ems Canal. On April 10, Montgomery accelerated the pace of the advance to the Elbe, deciding to skirt the congested and heavily defended port of Bremen in favor of concentrating on a fast advance to the Elbe. In the first two weeks of April, the British Second Army suffered 7,665 casualties but took over 78,100 prisoners. As mentioned earlier, on April 14, the right wing

Advance in the north, April–May 1945

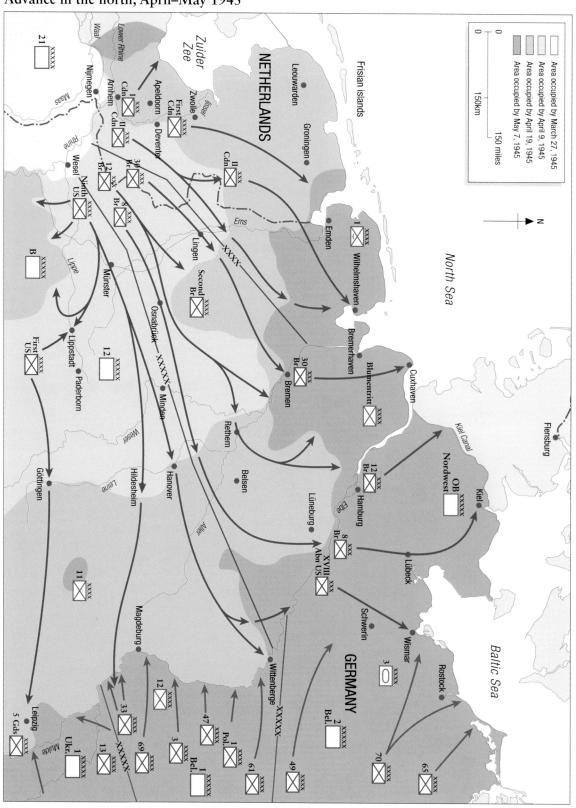

of the British Second Army began to encounter elements of the 12. Armee trying to reach the Harz Mountains, but these forces were quickly subdued and pushed southward into the American sector. The Elbe was reached on April 19 and steps were begun to deal with Bremen. Armee-Blumentritt attempted to defend Bremen using a variety of ad hoc formations, but this defense was overcome by 30 Corps late on April 26. In the meantime, the First Canadian Army began its operation to liberate the Netherlands. The initial thrust by Canadian II Corps pushed north along the Dutch–German frontier and the majority of the country was liberated by the third week of April.

Churchill was keen that Denmark be liberated by the western Allies and not by the Red Army since it controlled access to the Baltic. Following the envelopment of the Ruhr, Montgomery and Eisenhower came to agreement to free the 21st Army Group from the need to clear the Elbe in lower Saxony south of Wittenberge. Instead, the focus of the British Second Army would be Schleswig-Holstein, reaching the Baltic, and preventing a Soviet occupation of Denmark. During a meeting with Eisenhower on April 20, Montgomery expressed concern about a shortage of forces since the Ninth US Army had been returned to Bradley, so Eisenhower transferred Ridgway's XVIII Airborne Corps to his command.

The campaign to reach the Baltic, codenamed Operation *Enterprise*, was launched in the early morning hours of April 29 with crossings over the Elbe by 8 Corps near Lauenberg, 12 Corps over the Elbe near Hamburg and 30 Corps over the Weser near Bremen. Ridgway's XVIII Airborne Corps launched its advance a day later due to its prolonged road march into this sector, and its advance was aimed at Wismar and the Baltic. In spite of its name, Ridgway's corps was a combined-arms group including the 82nd Airborne Division, 8th Infantry Division, and 7th Armored Division. The last major German defensive concentration in northern Germany was the 1. Fallschirm-Armee around Hamburg reinforced by a hodge-podge of other units. The British 12 Corps began their assault on the city on April 28 and fighting concluded in five days.

Operation *Enterprise* proved to be a far less costly mission than originally feared. After word of Hitler's suicide was broadcast on May 1, most German soldiers and sailors showed little enthusiasm to continue fighting. The British 5th and 11th Armoured Divisions raced to Lubeck against little opposition to seal off Denmark. In Ridgway's sector, Gen. Kurt von Tippelskirch surrendered the entire 21. Armee, about 150,000 troops. In total the corps accepted the surrender of 359,960 German troops.

Rokossovskiy's 2nd Belorussian Front met Montgomery's 21st Army Group near Wismar in May 1945. The two commanders and their staffs met in the city

Although Churchill had feared that the Red Army might reach Denmark first, Rokossovskiy's progress had been slow. Manteuffel's 3. Panzer-Armee threw in its last major reserves against the 2nd Belorussian Front on April 26, but was so battered that it was forced to withdraw back to the Uecker River near Prenzlau after dark. Soviet tank columns began to race past the threadbare German defenses, and by April 27, the 3. Panzer-Armee had been routed. Manteuffel compared the situation to 1918 with thousands of German troops ignoring orders and heading west to avoid capture by the Red Army. On April 28, Keitel met with Manteuffel and Heinrici in hopes of staunching the flow. The situation had been made all the worse by the massive wave of frightened civilians on the roads that made tactical movement difficult or impossible. Heinrici, infuriated by Keitel's delusional schemes to stage a last-ditch stand in the north, was relieved of command of Armeegruppe Weichsel in the early morning hours of April 29. Under the circumstances, it made absolutely no difference.

The progress of Rokossovskiy's 2nd Belorussian Front accelerated due to the German collapse. The Soviet 70th Army, spearheaded by the 3rd Guards Tank Corps, raced for the Baltic and met the British Second Army near Wismar while the 49th Army met British forces further south on the Elbe.

THE NATIONAL REDOUBT

While the First US Army and Ninth US Army remained idle once reaching the demarcation line along Elbe, Eisenhower ordered Devers' 6th Army Group and Patton's Third US Army to continue to push southward through Bavaria and into Austria to pre-empt a last-ditch defense in the Alpine stronghold. The French were assigned the clearance of the Black Forest area while the Seventh US Army headed for Munich and the Austrian frontier.

Opposing them was Heeresgruppe G commanded by Gen. der Infanterie Friedrich Schulz. By mid-April 1945, Heeresgruppe G had been critically weakened and had no significant reserves. The supply situation was so hopeless that the army group headquarters was unable to make its planned move to the Nuremburg area due to a lack of fuel. To create a mobile counterattack force, the army group combed the Grafenwöhr training grounds and nearby factories, locating only 35 operational tanks. Together with two battalions of infantry, these were used to create Gruppe Grafenwöhr. This ragtag formation was assigned to defend Nuremburg on April 16 but was overrun by the 14th Armored Division. The main defense of the city was its belt of heavy flak guns. The collapse of the German defenses in Nuremburg on April 19 removed the entire right wing of 1. Armee and

The 1ere Armée Française enveloped the 19. Armee in the Black Forest region of southern Germany in April 1945. This is a French Foreign Legion M5 half-track of the Régiment de marche de la Légion étrangère, 5e Division Blindée. (NARA)

Advance in the south, April 24–May 11, 1945

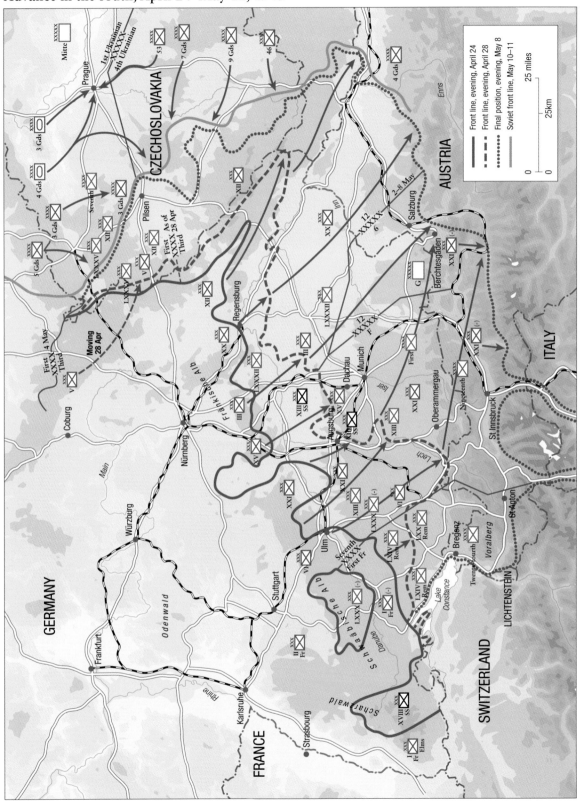

opened the door for the Seventh US Army to advance nearly 80km to the Danube, with XXI Corps crossing the river on April 21 near Dillingen. The collapse of the 1. Armee was also exploited by Patton's Third Army which advanced southeast in the final week of April, reaching the Danube near Regensburg on April 24.

De Lattre's 1ere Armée Française trapped the 19. Armee to the east of the Rhine in the Black Forest. Although Stuttgart had been assigned to the Seventh US Army, the French captured it on April 22 due to instructions from Paris. Devers faced growing problems in controlling de Lattre's force since de Gaulle's government wanted to create a French occupation zone within Germany before it had been sanctioned by Britain and the United States. After the capture of Stuttgart, the 1ere Armée Française pushed on to Ulm where the collaborationist Vichy French government had set up a puppet government-in-exile.

Patch's Seventh US Army and Patton's Third US Army continued their mechanized advance beyond the Danube during the final week of April 1945. A Seventh US Army report described the German defenses as follows:

> that of isolated groups, scattered and without organization, fighting with varying degrees of resistance. Inadequate distribution of what remained of his troops and scarcity of transport forced the enemy to defend fiercely at points where he could organize, leaving other and sometimes more important points lightly held. The result was armored spearheads slashing deep into the enemy's rear… At time the pursuit seemed more like a fantasy of violence, speed and extravagant incident. Armored columns were rolling 20 and 30 miles a day. Weakly-held strong points were destroyed by fire and huge enemy groups were shipped to the rear in bulk prisoner formations.

A handful of fresh German divisions attempted to stem the tide but were crushed. The new Division "Nibelungen" was deployed against the US III Corps near Ingolstadt on 27 April and was destroyed in three days of fighting.

The fighting in Bavaria also revealed the first faint signs of an anti-Nazi resistance. Civilian groups attempted to stage a coup in Augsburg shortly before the surrender of the city. Civilian groups did revolt in Munich, but it took street fighting by the US 3rd and 45th divisions to overcome a Waffen-SS Kaserne there on April 29–30.

After clearing Bavaria to the Alps by the end of April, Eisenhower instructed Devers' 6th Army Group to capture all the Alpine passes into Italy while Patton's Third Army was directed to Salzburg in Austria to capture the passes into the Austrian Tirol. As it transpired, Patton's attention was distracted further east, and Patch's Seventh US Army took Salzburg on May 4.

Patton's Third US Army was inundated with German prisoners, in many cases with entire divisions fleeing westward to avoid Soviet capture. From the renewal of the offensive on April 22 to the end of the war on May 8, Patton's Third US Army took an astonishing 765,483 prisoners. The collapse of the German 7. Armee prompted the Third US Army to continue over the German border into the Czech lands. Eisenhower had come to an agreement with the Red Army about moving into the western portion of the country as far as Plzen and České Budějovice, but when Patton requested permission to move as far as Prague, he was denied.

THE LIBERATION OF PRAGUE

The last major campaign in Europe in 1945 was the Prague operation. Stalin was concerned that the western Allies would push further eastward than outlined by the joint agreements and he became even more wary when Gen. Bradley offered to assist in the liberation of Czechoslovakia. On May 1, Stavka instructed Zhukov to relieve Konev's troops of their responsibilities in Berlin so that they could participate in the destruction of Heeresgruppe Mitte in the Czech lands. By this time, Schörner's forces numbered about 600,000 troops and were located primarily near Prague. The Stavka plan was for a hasty operation by Konev's 1st Ukrainian Front, Malinovskiy's 2nd Ukrainian Front and Gen. Yeremenko's 4th Ukrainian Front, totaling about two million troops. Starting on May 6, Konev's forces overran Dresden, Bautzen, and Gorlitz while the 4th Ukrainian Front took Olomouc. Schörner's intention was to conduct a westward withdrawal to surrender his troops to the Americans, conducting rearguard actions as necessary.

The initial Soviet plan was to start the Prague operation on May 7, but this was accelerated after Czech resistance forces staged an uprising in Prague on May 5 and called for help. On the night of May 8–9, Konev ordered the 3rd and 4th Tank Armies to make a dash for Prague. In spite of the surrender of the German government on the night of May 8–9, fighting continued in the Czech lands for several more days. The 2nd and 4th Ukrainian fronts reinforced Konev's forces in the fighting near Prague on May 9–10. The 4th Tank Army sent a detachment to link up with the US Army and they met Patton's forces on May 11. German units continued to try to flee Soviet captivity, and Patton's Third US Army accepted a further 515,205 POWs on May 9–13.

The Czech insurgents in Prague seized a number of Jagdpanzer 38 (Hetzer) assault guns manufactured at the ČKD plant in the outskirts of Prague. They were prominently marked with Czech flags and slogans.

The T-34-85 from the 3rd Guards Tank Army, 1st Ukrainian Front with infantry aboard enters Budyně nad Ohří on the approaches to Prague in May 1945. This unit had been involved in the storming of Berlin, but was hastily redirected to advance on Czechoslovakia.

The first Soviet tank into Prague was this one, number 1-24 commanded by Lt. I. G. Goncharenko, of the 63rd Guards Tank Brigade, 10th Guards Tank Corps, on the morning of May 9, 1945 before it was knocked out during the fighting.

This Jagdpanzer 38 was involved in one of the most famous tank duels of the Prague uprising, knocking out Goncharenko's T-34-85 before being knocked out in turn by other tanks of Goncharenko's unit. In the background is the famous Pražský hrad, Prague's royal castle.

ENDING THE WAR

The Yalta agreements had stipulated that Britain, the United States, and the Soviet Union would refrain from reaching any separate peace treaty with Germany but several regional armistices took place in early May 1945, including an armistice in Italy on May 2.

Hitler's death did not lead to an immediate surrender. His appointed successor, Grand Admiral Karl Dönitz, hoped to negotiate more favorable terms than unconditional surrender. His objective was to end the war with Britain and the United States as quickly as possible, but to continue to fight the Soviet Union and to permit more German civilians and soldiers to flee Soviet captivity. There was still a sizeable contingent of troops in the Kurland pocket who were being evacuated across the Baltic and there were hundreds of thousands of Germans fleeing westward every day. Dönitz and the OKW had already been forced to relocate on the night of May 2–3 due to British advances, and they ended up at the Marineschule Mürwik naval academy near Flensberg. Due to the chaotic conditions in northern Germany, Reichspräsident Dönitz did not create his new government until May 5. The likelihood increased daily that approaching British troops would capture his government.

Finally recognizing the hopelessness of the situation, Dönitz dispatched his Kriegsmarine successor, Admiral Hans-Georg von Friedeburg, to negotiate with the British. Montgomery made it clear that surrender was "necessary and not negotiable." As a result, Friedeburg signed surrender documents at 1800hrs on May 4 at Montgomery's headquarters, establishing a ceasefire in the Netherlands, northern Germany, and Denmark. Friedeburg was then obliged to fly to the SHAEF headquarters at Reims to meet Eisenhower in an

An initial surrender was signed on May 4 at the headquarters tent of the 21st Army Group on the Timeloberg hill at Wendisch Evern covering German forces in the Netherlands, northern Germany, and Denmark. Field Marshal Bernard Montgomery watches as the document is signed by Dönitz's representative, Admiral Hans-Georg von Friedeburg. (NARA)

The German delegation arrives at Zhukov's headquarters at Karlhorst in Berlin for the final surrender ceremony on the night of May 8–9, 1945. From left to right, Luftwaffe chief Generaloberst Hans-Jürgen Stumpff, chief of the OKW, Generalfeldmarschall Wilhelm Keitel, and head of the Kreigsmarine, Admiral Hans-Georg von Friedeburg. (NARA)

attempt to secure a similar ceasefire in the American sectors on the Rhine and in southern Germany. Eisenhower briskly rebuffed this ploy and made it clear that the only acceptable agreement was an unconditional surrender in both the west and the east. To buy time, Dönitz insisted on dispatching the head of the OKW, Gen. Alfred Jodl, to Reims on May 6. Jodl again tried to win a separate surrender agreement with the western Allies, but Eisenhower threatened that if the German did not immediately agree to an unconditional surrender, he would authorize the resumption of bomber attacks on German

As Dönitz's representative, Generaloberst Alfred Jodl signed the instruments of surrender at Eisenhower's SHAEF headquarters in Reims on May 8. To his left is his OKW aide and translator Major Wilhelm Oxenius and to his right is head of the Kreigsmarine, Admiral Hans-Georg von Friedeburg. (NARA)

cities and would also instruct all field commanders to shut off any further transit of German soldiers and civilians into areas under British and American control. At 0241hrs on May 7, Jodl signed the instrument of surrender at SHAEF headquarters in Reims, ending the war at midnight on May 8–9.

The Soviet representative at SHAEF, Gen. Ivan Susloparov, did not have clear instructions from Moscow, but signed the document with the caveat that the Soviet Union had the right to renegotiate the terms at a later date. Moments later, he received a telegram from Moscow instructing him not to sign. To paper over the matter, a second ceremony was staged at Zhukov's headquarters in the Karlshorst area of Berlin at 0016hrs, May 9 in Berlin.

Dönitz announced the surrender by radio on May 8 with the ceasefire to take place at 2300hrs. Due to the chaos, fighting dragged on for several days in the more distant theaters. The most intense fighting continued around Prague, lasting well into May 11; a ceasefire did not occur until May 15 in Yugoslavia. Curiously enough, one of the last battles was fought in the Netherlands. Georgian troops serving in the Wehrmacht on Texel Island mutinied against their German officers on the night of April 5–6. Heeresgruppe H sent reinforcements from the mainland, and a series of violent battles broke out between the Georgian troops and allied Dutch resistance fighters against Wehrmacht units. Canadian troops did not arrive on the island until May 20, bringing an end to the bloodshed.

THE CAMPAIGN IN PERSPECTIVE

The darkest nightmare of Hitler and the Nazi regime was a recurrence of the military collapse in November 1918 and the ensuing chaos and civil war in Germany. The leadership of the German armed forces largely absorbed this viewpoint and their shortsighted focus on the army's "honor" in avoiding this particular calamity made them blind to the possibilities of an even more dreadful end to the Third Reich. By needlessly prolonging the war long after any hope of victory had disappeared, the army leaders were complicit with Hitler for the bloody Gotterdammerung of 1945.

German military casualties during the "*Endkämpfe*" in 1945 have been estimated by German historian Rüdiger Overmans as 1.23 million of the 4.8 million dead and missing during the entire war. It was the most costly five

Soviet and American forces established a demarcation line in Austria shortly after the German surrender. Here, Maj. Gen. Horace McBride, commander of the 80th Infantry Division, of Patton's Third US Army, reviews Red Army troops including a T-34-85 tank alongside Gen. Maj. Pavel Voskresenskiy, 21st Rifle Division, 30th Rifle Corps, 26th Army, 3rd Ukrainian Front near Liezen on May 11, 1945. (NARA)

months of the long war. German civilian deaths in 1945 due to the ground campaigns have been estimated at over 170,000 due to the enormous loss of life in the chaotic evacuations from the eastern provinces. There were a further 82,000 dead from the bombing campaign in February–May 1945, bringing total German civilian war deaths in 1945 to over a quarter of a million. At the same time, the Nazi regime caused the deaths of tens of thousands of foreign forced laborers and concentration camp inmates in final acts of barbarity in 1945.

The ferocity of war differed dramatically between east and west. The Red Army was intent on revenge for the savage years of German occupation. War in eastern Germany was without mercy, and the defeated enemy was as apt to be killed as taken prisoner. During the Berlin operation, the Red Army estimated it captured 519,284 prisoners and killed 538,380 German troops for a POW/KIA ratio of 0.96:1. By comparison, Patton's Third Army estimated it had taken 332,904 prisoners and killed about 137,000 German troops in April 1945 or a POW/KIA ratio of 2.39:1. The Third US Army's estimate of the number of enemy soldiers killed is a gross exaggeration, and the actual POW/KIA ratio was probably more than 5:1. Regardless of the precise figures, it was far more likely that a surrendering German soldier would be taken alive as a prisoner in the west than in the east.

An enormous mass of German troops from Heeresgruppe Mitte and other units moved out of the Czech lands to escape Soviet captivity in May 1945. This is an assembly area for German troops set up by the US 1st Infantry Division in Eger (Czech: Cheb) in the Sudetenland on the Czech frontier near Nuremburg. The German supply cart in the foreground is marked Köln (Cologne) to serve as a meeting point for German enlisted men being sent back to that city. (NARA)

The western armies were much more casualty averse than their Soviet allies, preferring to use firepower over manpower. Army casualties of the western Allies in Europe in 1945 totaled about 318,000 including 60,000 dead. Soviet casualties in 1945 were 2.8 million including 631,633 dead, a cost about ten times as high.

Following Hitler's suicide, Dönitz's new government had few military options. The only effort with any consequence was their deliberate delay of the war's end in May 1945 to minimize the number of German troops and civilians falling into Red Army hands. This succeeded as well as could be expected under the circumstances. Of the 11.1 million German prisoners of war, 7.7 million fell into American, British, or French hands compared to 3.3 million in Soviet custody. The Red Army accepted the surrender of only 1.9 million German troops in 1945 compared to the western Allies who captured about six million, three times as many. About half of these troops fled into US and British zones to avoid the Red Army.

For the Red Army, the 1945 fighting marked a long-awaited end to a long and costly war. The fighting was every bit as intense as previous years of the conflict, with quarterly casualties in 1945 averaging 1.05 million compared to 0.97 million in 1943 and 0.83 million in 1944. German historians estimate that the Red Army accounted for about two-thirds of the casualties inflicted on the German Army in 1945. The Red Army victory in 1945 remains the central event in the Soviet era of Russian history, in no small measure due to the enormous human cost, in excess of 26 million dead.

Germany was in turmoil through 1945 due to massive dislocation of civilians fleeing the war zones. This is a scene in Bamberg shortly after the war's end as families attempt to return home. (NARA)

Red Army casualties in 1945 by campaign

Campaign	Period	Lost	Injured	Total
Vistula–Oder offensive	12 January–3 February	43,251	149,874	193,125
West Carpathian offensive	12–18 February	16,337	62,651	78,988
East Pomeranian offensive	10 February–4 April	52,740	172,952	225,962
Vienna Offensive	16 March–15 April	38,661	129,279	167,940
Berlin Offensive	16 April–8 May	78,291	274,184	352,475
Prague Offensive	6–11 May	11,265	38,083	49,348
Other	1 January–8 May	391,088	1,364,725	1,755,543
Total	1 January–8 May	631,633	2,191,748	2,823,381

By the spring of 1945, the conflicting war aims of the Soviet Union and its Anglo-American allies were coming into sharper focus. The coalition that had so successfully prosecuted the war against Germany lasted only a few years before degenerating into a half-century of Cold War. Grim memories of the grotesque violence of 1945 helped dissuade the new rivals from ever letting the Cold War turn hot.

THE BATTLEFIELD TODAY

Germany does not commemorate the Third Reich except as penance for past sins. There are no battlefield museums commemorating the Wehrmacht but there are somber museums at several of the concentration camps such as Dachau and Nordhausen. A number of buildings closely associated with the Nazi regime, such as the new Reich Chancellery, were demolished. Vestiges of other wartime buildings such as the ruins of the Humboldthain Flak tower still remain. Tony Le Tissier has guidebooks to Berlin which identify these many sites. Sites in Pomerania, Silesia, and Prussia are now outside Germany due to post-war border changes. Küstrin is now the Polish town of Kostrzyn; Königsberg is now the Russian city of Kaliningrad.

The Soviet Army erected numerous monuments in occupied East Germany to celebrate Soviet victories in 1945. These can still be seen in many locations such as Berlin and the Seelow Heights. Many artifacts from the 1945 fighting, especially the Berlin campaign, can be found in Russian military museums. There is a virtual altar to the 1945 victory in the Central Museum of the Armed Forces in Moscow, with captured bits of Nazi regalia as its sacred relics.

Soviet memorials have not fared as well at other sites of the 1945 fighting. For example, the Soviet Army erected a massive pedestal on Štefánik square in Prague with an IS-2m heavy tank commemorating the first Soviet tank into the city, Goncharenko's T-34-85. It was widely reviled as a symbol of Soviet oppression and after the 1989 Velvet Revolution it was vandalized repeatedly, often painted pink. In frustration, the Czech government finally moved it to a less provocative location at the Lešany military museum.

The victory over Germany in May 1945 is widely celebrated in museums of the former Soviet Union. The Central Armed Forces Museum in Moscow has a large exhibit hall celebrating the 1945 victory including this plexiglass case filled with Iron Crosses taken from German prisoners-of-war and a bronze imperial eagle that had been above the entrance door to Ehrenhof courtyard at the Reich Chancellery.

FURTHER READING

There is extensive coverage of the final campaigns including the official US Army history by MacDonald, and the corresponding British history by Ellis. The Soviet General Staff study of the Berlin operation was released in an annotated form under Goncharov's editorship in 2007. The tenth volume of the semi-official German history of the war, *Das Deutsche Reich und der Zweite Weltkrieg* has not yet been translated into English by Oxford, though it presumably will be at some future date. One of the names most closely associated with the Berlin fighting is Tony Le Tissier, who has a number of excellent accounts covering various aspects of the campaign. The list here contains only a small fraction of the books and studies covering this final campaign.

Unpublished Government Studies

Bauer, Magna, *The End of Army Group Weichsel and Twelfth Army 27 April–7 May 1945* (FMS R-69: 1956)

Geyer, Rolf, *Army Group H: 10 Mar–9 May 1945* (FMS B-414: 1946)

Glantz, David (ed.), *From the Vistula to the Oder: Soviet Offensive Operations October 1944–March 1945, Transcript of Proceedings 1986 Art of War Symposium* (US Army War College: 1986)

Hohne, Gustav, *Final Operations of Army Blumentritt: 10 April–5 May 1945* (FMS B-361: 1951)

Reichelm, Günther, *The Last Rally: Battles Fought by the German 12 Army in the Heart of Germany, Between East and West: 13 April–7 May 1945* (FMS B-606: 1947)

Willemer, Wilhelm, et al., *The German Defense of Berlin* (FMS P-136: 1954)

Wilutzky, Horst, *The Fighting of Heeresgruppe G in the West: The Final Battle in Central and Southern Germany until the Surrender 22 May–6 May 1945* (FMS B-703: 1947)

n.a., *Boevoy sostav sovetskoy armii 1941–1945* (Military Academic Directorate of the Soviet Army General Staff: 1963)

Books

Ambrose, Stephen, *Eisenhower and Berlin 1945: The Decision to Halt at the Elbe* (W. W. Norton: 1967)

Beevor, Anthony, *The Fall of Berlin 1945* (Viking: 2002)

Bergstrom, Christer, *Bagration to Berlin: The Final Air Battles in the East 1944–45* (Classic: 2008)

Bettinger, Dieter, *Die Geschichte der Heeresgruppe G: Mai 1944 bis Mai 1945* (Helios: 2010)

Delaforce, Patrick, *Invasion of the Third Reich: Operation Eclipse* (Amberly: 2011)

Ellis, L. F. and A. E. Warhurst, *Victory in the West, Vol. 2: The Defeat of Germany* (HMSO: 1968)

Erickson, John, *The Road to Berlin: Stalin's War with Germany, Vol. 2* (Weidenfeld and Nicolson: 1983)

Fritz, Stephen, *Endkampf: Soldiers, Civilians and the Death of the Third Reich* (University Press of Kentucky: 2004)

Glantz, David, *What If? On to Berlin: The Allied Advance on Hitler's Lair, April 1945* (Self-published: 2006)

Glantz, David and Jonathan House, *When Titans Clashed: How the Red Army Stopped Hitler* (University Press of Kansas: 1995)

Goncharov, V. (ed), *Bitva za Berlin: Zavershayushcheye srazhenie VOV* (AST: 2007)

Guckelhorn, Wolfgang, *Das Ende am Rhein: Kriegsende zwischen Remagen und Andernach* (Helios: 2005)

Hamilton, Stephan, *The Oder Front 1945: Gen.Obst. Gotthard Heinrici, HG Weichsel and Germany's Final Defense in the East, 20 Mar–3 May 1945* (Helion: Vol. 1, 2011; Vol 2, 2014)

Isayev, Aleksey, *Berlin 45-go: Srazheniya v logove zverya* (AST: 2014)

Konev, Ivan, *Year of Victory* (Progress: 1969)

Jakl, Tomas, *May 1945 in the Czech Lands: Ground Operations of the Axis and Allied Forces* (MBI: 2004)

Lakowski, Richard, *Seelow 1945: Die Entscheidungsschlacht an der Oder* (Mittler: 2013)

Le Tissier, Tony, *The Battle of Berlin 1945* (St Martin's: 1988)

Le Tissier, Tony, *Berlin: Battlefield Guide, Third Reich and Cold War* (Pen & Sword: 2014)

Le Tissier, Tony, *The Siege of Küstrin: Gateway to Berlin, 1945* (Pen & Sword: 2009)

Le Tissier, Tony, *Zhukov at the Oder: The Decisive Battle for Berlin* (Praeger: 1996)

Longacre, Edward, *War in the Ruins: The American Army's Final Battle against Nazi Germany* (Westholme: 2010)

MacDonald, Charles, *The European Theater of Operations: The Last Offensive* (US Army Center of Military History: 1973)

Malinovskiy, Rodion, *Budapesht, Vena, Praga* (Nauka: 1965)

Mierzejewski, Alfred, *The Collapse of the German War Economy 1944–45* (University of North Carolina: 1988)

Minott, Rodney, *The Fortress that Never Was: The Myth of Hitler's Bavarian Stronghold* (Holt, Rinehart & Winston: 1964)

Müller, Rolf-Dieter (ed.), *Das Deutsche Reich und der Zweite Weltkrieg, Band 10/1: Der Zusammenbruch des Deutschen Reiches 1945* (Deutsche Verlags-Anstalt: 2008)

Overmans, Rüdiger, *Soldaten hinter Stacheldraht: Deutsche Kriegsgefangene des Zweiten Weltkriege* (Ullstein: 2000)

Ryan, Cornelius, *The Last Battle* (Simon & Schuster: 1966)

Scherer, Wingolf, *Vergeblicher Widerstand: Das Ende der Heeresgruppe B zweischen Rhein, Ruhr und Sieg* (Helios: 2007)

Shein, Dmitriy, *Tanki vedet Rybalko: Boevoy put 3-y Gvardeyskoy tankovoy armii* (Yauza: 2007)

Shtemenko, Semyon, *The Last Six Months* (Doubleday: 1977)

Tieke, Wilhelm, *Das Ende zwischen Oder und Elbe- Der Kampf um Berlin 1945* (Motorbuch: 1992)

Yelton, David, *Hitler's Volkssturm: The Nazi Militia and the Fall of Germany 1944–45* (University Press of Kansas: 2002)

Zumbro, Derek, *Battle for the Ruhr: the German Army's Final Defeat in the West* (University Press of Kansas: 2006)

INDEX

Note: page numbers in **bold** refer to illustrations, captions and plates.